The Earth

SonLight Education Ministry
United States of America

A Suggested Daily Schedule

(Adapt this schedule to your family needs.)

5:00 a.m.  Arise–Personal Worship

6:00 a.m. Family Worship and Bible Class–With Father

7:00 a.m. Breakfast

8:00 a.m. Practical Arts*–Domestic Activities
                         Agriculture
                         Industrial Arts
                         (especially those related to
                         the School Lessons)

10:00 a.m. School Lessons
(Take a break for some physical exercise
during this time slot.)

12:00 p.m. Dinner Preparations
(Health class could be included at this time
or a continued story.)

1:00 p.m. Dinner

2:00 p.m. Practical Arts* or Fine Arts
(Music and Crafts)
(especially those related to
the School Lessons)

5:00 p.m. Supper

6:00 p.m. Family Worship–Father
(Could do History Class)

7:00 p.m. Personal time with God–Bed Preparation

8:00 p.m. Bed

*Daily nature walk can be in morning or afternoon.

The Desire of All Nations

This book is a part of a curriculum that is built upon the life of Christ entitled, "The Desire of All Nations," for grades 2-8. Any of the books in this curriculum can be used by themselves or as an entire program.

INFORMATION ABOUT THE 2-8 GRADE PROGRAM

Multi-level

This program is written on a multi-level. That means that each booklet has material for grades 2-8. This is so the whole family in these grades may work from the same books. It is difficult for a busy mother to have 2 or more children and each have a different set of books. Remember, the Bible is written for all ages.

The Bible—the Primary Textbook

The books in this program are designed to teach the parent and the student how to learn academic subjects by using the Bible as a primary textbook.

The Desire of Ages

The Desire of Ages by Ellen G. White is used as a textbook to go with the Bible. This focuses on the early life of Christ, when He was a child. Children relate best to Christ as a child and youth.

Lesson Numbers

The big number in the top right corner on the cover of this book is the Lesson Number and corresponds with the chapter number in the book *The Desire of Ages*. For example, Lesson 1 in the school program will go along with chapter 1 in *The Desire of Ages*. Usually each family starts at the beginning with Lesson 1. Most children have not had a true Bible program, therefore they need the foundation built. If there is academic material that they have already covered, they do the Bible part and review then pass quickly on.

Seven Academic Subjects

There are seven academic subjects in this program—Health, Mathematics, Music, Science–Nature, History/Geography/Prophecy, Language, Voice–Speech.

Language Program

A good, solid language program is recommended to be used along with the SonLight materials.

The Riggs Institute has a multi-sensory teaching method that accommodates every child's unique learning style. Their program is called *Writing and Spelling Road to Reading and Thinking*. Order by calling (800) 200-4840 or visit www.riggsinst.org. (Disclaimer: SonLight does not endorse the reading books recommended in the Riggs' program.)

Another option which you might find more user friendly and is similar to the Riggs program but from a Christian perspective is *Spell to Write and Read* by Wanda Sanseri. To order, call Wanda Sanseri at (503) 654-2300 or visit https://www.bhibooks.net/swr.html

"God's Chosen People"
Lesson 2 – Diligence

**The following books are those you will need for this lesson.
All of these can be obtained from www.sonlighteducation.com**

The Rainbow Covenant – Study the spiritual meaning of colors and make your own rainbow book.

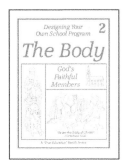

Health
The Body

Math
A Place

Music
What Makes Sound?

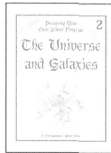

Science/Nature
The Universe and Galaxies

A Casket – Coloring book and story. Learn how to treat the gems of the Bible.

H/G/P
The Earth

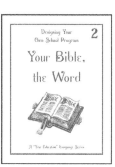

Language
Your Bible, the Word

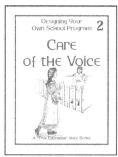

Speech/Voice
Care of the Voice

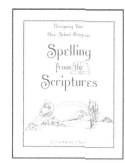

Spelling from the Scriptures

Bible Study – Learn how to study the Bible and helpful use tools.

Bible
*The Desire of all Nations I
Teacher Study Guide*

Student Study Guide

Bible Lesson Study Guide

Memory Verses
*The Desire of all Nations I
Scripture Songs Book*

and MP3 files

Our Nature Study Book – Your personal nature journal.

Table of Contents

Go Ye Into All the World

"The Lord hath made known his salvation:
his righteousness hath he openly shown
in the sight of the heathen.

"He hath remembered his mercy and his truth
toward the house of Israel:
all the ends of the earth have seen
the salvation of our God."

Psalm 98:2-3

The great salvation wrought by Him
Jehovah has made known.
His justice in the nations' sight
He openly has shown.

He mindful of His grace and truth
To Isr'el's house has been.
The great salvation of our God
All ends of Earth have seen.

Missions

"The Saviour's words, *'Ye are the light of the world,'* point to the fact that He has committed to His followers a world-wide mission. In the days of Christ, selfishness and pride and prejudice had built strong and high the wall of partition between the appointed guardians of the sacred oracles and every other nation on the globe. But the Saviour and come to change all this. The words which the people were hearing from His lips were unlike anything to which they had ever listened from priest or rabbi. Christ tears away the wall of partition, the self-love, the dividing prejudice of nationality, and teaches a love for all the human family. He lifts men from the narrow circle that their selfishness prescribes; He abolishes all territorial lines and artificial distinctions of society. He makes no difference between neighbors and strangers, friends and enemies. He teaches us to look upon every needy soul as our neighbor and the world as our field.

"As the rays of the sun penetrate to the remotest corners of the globe, so God designs that the light of the gospel shall extend to every soul upon the Earth. If the church of Christ were fulfilling the purpose of our Lord, light would be shed upon all that sit in darkness and in the region and shadow of death. Instead of congregating together and shunning responsibility and cross bearing, the members of the church would scatter into all lands, letting the light of Christ shine out from them, working as He did for the salvation of souls, and this *'gospel of the kingdom'* would speedily be carried to all the world." (*The Mount of Blessing* 42-43)

Teacher Section

"He stretcheth out the north
over the empty place,
and hangeth the earth upon nothing."
Job 26:7

INSTRUCTIONS
For the Teacher

Step 1

Study the Bible Lesson and begin to memorize the Memory Verses. Familiarize Yourself With the Character Quality. The student can answer the Bible Review Questions. See page 6. Use the Steps in Bible Study.

Bible Lesson

God's Chosen People – Exodus 20:3-6; Psalm 115:4-8; Isaiah 43:1-11; 49:3-6; 56:7; Ezra 9:5-7; Romans 1:22-23

Memory Verses

Isaiah 56:7; Deuteronomy 26:18-19; 28:10; 4:5-6

Character Quality

Diligence – constant effort to accomplish what is undertaken; exertion of body or mind without unnecessary delay or sloth; due attention; industry

Antonyms – dilatoriness; slowness; casualness; slothfulness

Character Quality Verses

Colossians 3:23 – *"And whatsoever ye do, do it heartily, as to the Lord, and not unto men."*

Proverbs 4:23 –*"Keep thy heart with all **diligence**; for out of it are the issues of life."*

Step 2

Understand How To/And

A. Do the Spelling Cards so the student can begin to build his own spiritual dictionary.

B. Mark the Bible.

C. Evaluate Your Student's Character in relation to the character quality of **diligence**.

D. Familiarize Yourself With the Earth. Notice the Projects.

E. Study the Scripture References on the Earth. Use the concordance.

F. Notice the Answer Key.

A. Spelling Cards Spelling Lists

H/G/P Words
Place I - II - III
age
area
change (ed)
earth
inside
moon
outside
shape
size
world

Place II - III
crust
globe
gravity
motion
surface
weight

Place III
atmosphere
continent
chemical makeup
movements
planet

Bible Words*
chosen
covenant
diligence
fools
glorified
graven
idols
image
iniquities
jealous
light
likeness
professing
restore
servant
serve
trespass
witnesses
wise

sphere
temperature

*See *The Desire of Ages Study Guide* for a more comprehensive spelling list.

See the booklet
Spelling from the Scriptures
for instructions about
how to make
the Spelling Cards.

B. How to Mark the Bible

1. Copy the list of Bible texts in the back of the Bible on an empty page as a guide.

2. Go to the first text in the Bible and copy the next text beside it. Go to the next one and repeat the process until they are all chain-referenced.

3. Have the student present the study to family and/or friends.

4. In each student lesson there is a section that has a Mark Your Bible on the subject studied. (See the Student's Section, page 75.)

C. Evaluate Your Student's Character

This section is for the purpose of helping the teacher know how to encourage the students in becoming more **diligent**.

See page 7.

Place I = Grades 2-3-4
Place II = Grades 4-5-6
Place III = Grades 6-7-8

D. Familiarize Yourself With The Earth – Notice the Projects

Projects

1. As a family do a missionary activity, such as handing out tracts on Christ's Second Coming. Be **diligent**!

2. Have the child give a verbal report of current world news. (Parents will need to screen this carefully.)

3. Look at a world map and notice how many continents there are on planet Earth. Learn to correctly pronounce their names and find them on a world map.

4. Read with the student Psalm 24:1. The child can copy the verse beneath a picture of the Earth the child has found. Find a cross reference to Psalm 24:1.

5. Help the child draw a picture of the Earth in the Milky Way Galaxy.

6. Read the chapter "The Creation" in the book *Patriarchs and Prophets*.

7. Go on a nature walk and find some of the beautiful riches that God filled the Earth with.

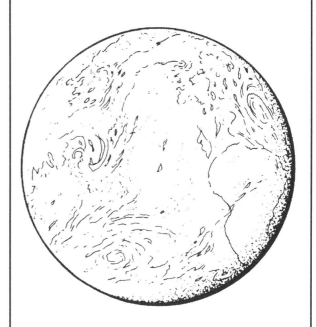

God made the Earth

"God made the Earth
and filled it with riches
and beauty
for man
to dwell in."

—Daniel March

E. Review the Scripture References for "The Earth"

Teacher, read the section on "Earth" in the *Strong's Concordance* before working on the lesson with the student.

F. Notice the Answer Key

The Answer Key for the student book is found on page 8.

Step 3

Read the Lesson Aim.

Lesson Aim

The aim of this lesson is to teach your student that God has chosen him to be part of His people today. Planet Earth became the battle ground for sin. His people of the past were not **diligent** to know and do His will.

We need to be **diligent** and be led by God day by day.

The Milky Way Galaxy, one of the many billions of galaxies in the universe, is one solar system with one little planet in rebellion against God. That is planet Earth.

God chose a body of people that He might teach and train them. They would represent Him and prepare the world for His first coming. The children of Israel lost the meaning of the symbols which God gave to show them the way of salvation through Christ Jesus.

God has again in these end days chosen a body of people on planet Earth, to prepare the world for His second coming. They, like Israel of old, have not been **diligent** in the study of the Word, and have lost the meaning of the symbols.

Today, the work of His body of people is to bring reform to the church and the world, that the last demonstration of His glory on this Earth may be seen before He comes the second time.

Were the Jewish nation ready to meet Jesus at His first coming? Are you prepared as a family to meet Him for His second coming?

Step 4

Prepare to begin the Earth Lesson.

To Begin The Earth Lesson

Show the child a globe and make it spin. Discuss the Earth God created in 6 days.

Step 5

These lessons are designed for the whole family. Begin the Earth lesson. Cover only what can be understood by your student. Make the lessons a family project by all being involved in part or all of them.

Steps in Bible Study

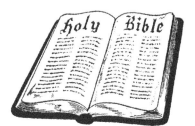

1. Prayer

2. Read the verses/meditate/memorize.

3. Look up key words in *Strong's Concordance* and find their meaning in the Hebrew or Greek dictionary in the back of that book.

4. Cross reference (marginal reference) with other Bible texts. An excellent study tool is *The Treasury of Scripture Knowledge.*

5. Use Bible custom books for more information on the times.

6. Write a summary of what you have learned from those verses.

7. Mark key thoughts in the margin of your Bible.

8. Share your study with others to reinforce the lessons you have learned.

Review Questions

1. What religious worship prevailed anciently? (Romans 1:22, 23; Psalm 115:4-8)

2. What was the great mission of the chosen people, Israel? (Exodus 20:3-6; Isaiah 43:10, 11; 49:3-6; 56:7)

3. How did they fail in their duty? (Ezra 9:5-7)

4. Thought Question: How did God overrule Israel's failure for the accomplishment of His purpose and their mission?

5. What three nations or races were most influential in the civilized world at the time of Christ? For what was each remarkable? (a. Rome–Law; b. Greeks–Language; c. Jews–Religion)

6. What had each contributed to prepare the way for the spread of the gospel?

(a. Rome – Government; b. Greek – Language; c. Jews – Knowledge of the true God)

7. God prepared the Gentile world for the coming of the Redeemer by:

a. System of heathenism had lost its hold on the people

b. Bible had been translated into Greek and was the universal language

c. Some Jews remained steadfast and true to the true God.

D. Palestine was the center of the world's gatherings.

8. Who is God's chosen people today? (His faithful followers)

Questions 5, 6 and 7 will need to be asked and then answered by the teacher.

Evaluating Your Child's Character

Check the appropriate box for your student's level of development,
or your own, as the case may be.

Maturing Nicely (MN), Needs Improvement (NI), Poorly Developed (PD), Absent (A)

Diligence

1. Does the student have difficulty in following through on assigned tasks without being reminded?

Yes ☐   No ☐

2. Does the student tend to take on the responsibilities of others, leaving his/her own responsibilities unattended?

Yes ☐   No ☐

3. Is the student able to complete tasks in spite of distractions?

Yes ☐   No ☐

4. Does the student need constant supervision in order to perform at their best level?

Yes ☐   No ☐

5. Is the time that a child can wait between achievement and reward increasing appreciably?

MN ☐ NI ☐ PD ☐ A ☐

6. Does the student move quickly and efficiently on the job, or does he move slowly?

MN ☐ NI ☐ PD ☐ A ☐

7. Does the student look forward to the job or complains about the task?

MN ☐ NI ☐ PD ☐ A ☐

8. Will the student first do the job to please the Lord and then his parents?

MN ☐ NI ☐ PD ☐ A ☐

Answer Key

Page 20

1. About 6,000 years

2. Teacher, check.

3. To be **diligent** in mission work

4. See page 12, 15, and 16. Page 1 has a picture of planet Earth.

5. Teacher, refer to the Bible Lesson.

6. Constant effort to accomplish what is undertaken; exertion of body or mind without unnecessary delay or sloth; due attention; industry.

Unwillingness to work or exert oneself; laziness; idleness. (Refer the student to a dictionary to define this word.)

7. Teacher, check.

8. Teacher, check.

Page 46

1. "If I practice one day, I can see the result; if I practice two days, my friends can see it; if three days, the great public can see it."

Page 46 continued

2. Walking with Christ. (Students may have various answers.)

3. No, every task should be done for Jesus and in doing this we would not be concerned about time, money, or effort.

4. Student read. Teacher discuss the information with him.

Page 50

1. Diameter is the distance through the center of an object. See page 21.

2. See pages 22-24.
Spins like a top spins; travels around the sun; and moves through the Milky Way as does the rest of the solar system.

3. Mr. Samuel Wesley an Anglican clergyman; Mrs. Susanna Wesley was a godly, dedicated mother, her son John Wesley, was the founder of the Methodist Church; Charles Wesley was also a founder of Methodism and shared its leadership with his brother John.

Page 50 continued

4. It is about 1/4 the size of Earth's diameter.

5. God shaped the Earth like a ball. It is not perfectly round. It is somewhat flat at the poles.

See page 42 for spiritual lessons.

6. The Earth's atmosphere is made up of 78 percent nitrogen, 21 percent oxygen, 1 percent argon, and small amounts of other gases.

See pages 48-49 for the spiritual lessons.

Page 54

1. North America
2. South America
3 Europe
4. Asia
5. Africa
6. Australia
7. Antarctica
(These can be written in any order.)

Page 55

They lacked a conversion experience. (Student may have various answers.)

Page 56

1. North America
2. Europe
3. Africa
4. Australia
5. South America
6. Antarctica
7. Asia

Page 59

1. Teacher, check.

2. The picture should be similar to the illustration on page 57.

3. Teacher do this exercise with the student.

4. Zion returns thanksgiving and praise to God for the wonderful favors bestowed upon her. God has graciously removed her shame and made her to appear glorious in the eyes of the world. These "garments" represent the perfect character of Christ that His people are to wear, even in this life. They stand in sharp contrast with our own "filthy rags." Sin has made the Earth desolate and waste, but it will not always remain so. The gospel of God's grace will cause the desert places to spring into bloom and to bear fruits of righteousness to the glory of God.

Page 73

1. Teacher, dictate the spelling words. The child should know not only how to spell the word but how to pronounce it, and the meaning of the word.

2. God created this world to enlarge heaven; to have a creation in His Own image; beings that could think, learn, understand, and appreciate His love. (The student's answer may vary from this one.)

3. Read Genesis 1 with the student.

4. Man was made in the image of God, he was to have dominion over the Earth; he was to be tested and if faithful would repopulate heaven to take the place of the angels that fell.

5. The Flood
(For a more detailed answer, see pages 63-66.)

6. Teacher, check.

7. By being **diligent** in being faithful to God in every area of our life. (Student's answer may vary from this one.)

Notes

Gardening Sheet

Lesson _____ Two _____ **Subject** <u>History/Geography/Prophecy</u>

Title _____ "The Earth" _____

In Season	Out of Season

Draw	**A**
Garden	**Plan**

Notes

In drawing out your plan be sure to note spacing of plants, maturity time, when to harvest, and when to plant afterwards.

Once you draw your plan take your calendar and mark when you plant and each successive planting. Notice the enclosed chart.

Remember, Ecclesiastes 3:2 says, *"A time to plant, and a time to pluck up that which is planted."* Israel was not **diligent** to know her time. Are you?

		First sowing as soon as ground is prepared		
Row	**Vegetable**	**Days to Harvest**	**Harvest lasts**	**Follow crop**
6	Beets	60 days	6 weeks	August 1, lettuce
2	Broccoli	70 days	To frost	one
7	Carrots	60 days	8 weeks	None
8	Endive, curly	70 days	6 weeks	August 10, beans
9	Endive, broad-leaved	90 days	6 weeks	None
10	Kale	60 days	To freeze	None
11	Lettuce	40 days	6 weeks	July 15, carrots
12	Onion sets	20 days	4 weeks	June 10, beans
13	Parsley	75 days	To freeze	None
14	Parsnips	95 days	To spring	None
15-16	Peas	64 days	2 weeks	Row 15, July 1, endive
				Row 16, July 1, onion seed for late green onions
26	New Zealand spinach	60 days	To freeze	None
3	Swiss chard	60 days	To freeze	None
17	Turnips	60 days	2 weeks	July 1, Chinese cabbage
		*Sow a week before frost proof day**		
18	Bush beans	60 days	4 weeks	August 10, beets
1-Fence	Pole lima beans	80 days	To frost	None
		*Sow or transplant when frost danger is over**		
19	Beets	60 days	6 weeks	None
20	Carrots	60 days	8 weeks	None
28-Fence	Cucumbers	45 days	6 weeks	Cucumbers
21	Lettuce	40 days	6 weeks	August 15, turnips
22	Onion sets	20 days	4 weeks	July 10, beans
27	Italian marrow	60 days	To frost	None
		Begin with well-started plants		
5	Eggplant	75 days	To frost	None
4	Peppers	60 days	To frost	None
Back fence	Early tomatoes	60 days		
Back fence	Late tomatoes	90 days	To frost	None
		Sow 60 days after first sowing		
23	Lettuce	40 days	6 weeks	None
25	Carrots	60 days	8 weeks	None
24	Beets	60 days	6 weeks	None

*Check with local county agent or weather bureau
to get date of last killing frost in your area.*

Music

"Here Am I; Send Me"

"But before that coming, Jesus said, *'This gospel of the kingdom shall be preached in all the world for a witness unto all nations'* (Matthew 24:14). His kingdom will not come until the good tidings of His grace have been carried to all the Earth. Hence, as we give ourselves to God, and win other souls to Him, we hasten the coming of His kingdom. Only those who devote themselves to His service, saying, *'Here am I; send me'* (Isaiah 6:8), to open blind eyes, to turn men *'from darkness to light and from the power of Satan unto God, that they may receive forgiveness of sins and inheritance among them which are sanctified'* (Acts 26:18)—they alone pray in sincerity, *'Thy kingdom come.'*"*

Thoughts From the Mount of Blessing 108-109

"This gospel of the kingdom shall be preached in all the world for a witness unto all nations."

Work, for the Night Is Coming

Mrs. Anna L. Coghill   Lowell Mason

1. Work, for the night is com - ing; Work through the morn - ing hours;
2. Work, for the night is com - ing; Work through the sun - ny noon;
3. Work, for the night is com - ing; Un - der the sun - set skies,

Work while the dew is spar - kling; Work 'mid spring - ing flowers;
Fill bright - est hours with la - bor, Rest comes sure and soon;
While their bright tints are glow - ing, Work, for day - light flies;

Work while the day grows bright - er, Un - der the glow - ing sun;
Give ev - ery fly - ing min - ute Some - thing to keep in store;
Work till the last beam fad - eth, Fad - eth to shine no more;

Work, for the night is com - ing, When man's work is done.
Work, for the night is com - ing, When man works no more.
Work while the night is dark - ening, When man's work is o'er.

I Would Be Like Jesus

James Row   B. D. Ackley

1. Earth - ly plea - sures vain - ly call me; I would be like Je - sus;
2. He has bro - ken ev - ery fet - ter, I would be like Je - sus;
3. All the way from earth to glo - ry, I would be like Je - sus;
4. That in heav - en He may meet me, I would be like Je - sus;
   would be like Je - sus;

Noth - ing world - ly shall en - thrall me; I would be like Je - sus.
That my soul may serve Him bet - ter, I would be like Je - sus.
Tell - ing o'er and o'er the sto - ry, I would be like Je - sus.
That His words "Well done" may greet me, I would be like Je - sus.
   would be like Je - sus.

Refrain

Be like Je - sus, this my song, In the home and in the throng;

Be like Je - sus, all day long! I would be like Je - sus.

From Greenland's Icy Mountains

Reginald Heber

Lowell Mason

1. From Green-land's i - cy moun- tains, From In - dia's cor - al strand,
2. What though the spic - y breez - es Blow soft o'er Cey-lon's isle;
3. Can men, whose souls are light - ed With wis - dom from on high,
4. Waft, waft, ye winds, His sto - ry, And you, ye wa-ters, roll,

Where Af - ric's sun - ny foun - tains Roll down their gold - en sands,
Though ev - ery pros-pect pleas - es, And on - ly man is vile;
Can they to men be - night - ed The lamp of life de - ny?
Till, like a sea of glo - ry, It spreads from pole to pole;

From man - y an an-cient riv - er, From man - y a palm - y plain,
In vain with lav - ish kind-ness The gifts of God are strewn;
Sal - va - tion! O sal - va - tion! The joy - ful sound pro - claim,
Till o'er our ran-somed na - ture The Lamb for sin - ners slain,

They call us to de - liv - er Their land from er - ror's chain.
The heath - en in his blind-ness Bows down to wood and stone.
Till earth's re - mot - est na - tion Has learned Mes - si - ah's name.
Re - deem - er, King, Cre - a - tor, In bliss re - turns to reign.

All Things Bright and Beautiful

Cecil F. Alexander

Adapted from an English
traditional melody
by Martin Shaw

1. All things bright and beau-ti-ful, All creatures great and small,

All things wise and won-der-ful, The Lord God made them all.

2. Each lit-tle flower that o-pens, Each lit-tle bird that sings;
3. The pur-ple-head-ed moun-tain, The riv-er run-ning by,
4. The cold wind in the win-ter, The pleasant summer sun,
5. He gave us eyes to see them, And lips that we might tell

He made their glow-ing col-ors, He made their ti-ny wings.
The sun-set, and the morn-ing That bright-ens up the sky,
The ripe fruits in the gar-den, He made them ev-ery one.
How great is God Al-might-y, Who has made all things well.

"Into All the World"

"The Lord gave the word:
great was the company
of those what published it."
Psalm 68:11

The LORD will give the word which He
    Commanded to be shown;
The people are a mighty host
    To make the tidings known.

Student Section

"Where wast thou when I laid the foundations of the earth?
declare, if thou hast understanding.

"Who hath laid the measures thereof, if thou knowest?
or who hath stretched the line upon it?

"Whereupon are the foundations thereof fastened?
or who laid the corner stone thereof...?"
Job 38:4-6

Continents – The Earth

Research
How Earth Began

"In the Beginning, God created the heaven and the earth."
Genesis 1:1

About 6,000 years ago God created the Earth to be inhabited by "His Chosen People." He never starts a project that He does not finish. He is **diligent** in all He does. "Infinite love—how great it is!" "God's creation is but a reservoir of means made ready for Him to employ instantly to do His pleasure." "All heaven took a deep and joyful interest in the creation of the world and of man. Human beings were a new and distinct order. They were made *'in the image of God,'* and it was the Creator's design that they should populate the Earth."*

Sin interrupted His perfect plan for planet Earth. However, through Christ coming to this world, sin will finally be removed from the universe. He says, *"And I saw a new heaven and a new earth, for the first heaven and the first earth were passed away; and there was no more sea"* (Revelation 21:1).

*1 Bible Commentary 1081

Reminder
Earth

The word Earth has four basic definitions which are:

1. The planet we live on;

2. Soil, dirt;

3. The land as different from the sea and the air; and

4. Sparsely populated land, which is one symbolic Bible definition, as in Revelation 12:16.

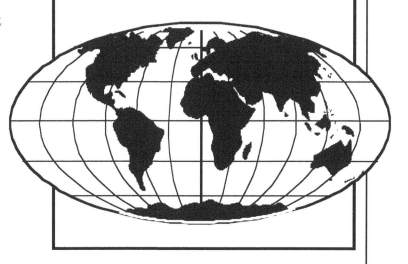

Are You a Sloth or a Beaver?
Are You <u>Diligent</u> or Slothful?

"Whatsoever ye do, do it heartily, as to the Lord, and not unto men."
Colossians 3:23

A sloth is a family of South America animals which have s–l–o–w and peculiar ways of moving. They never seem to be in a hurry to accomplish any task. While a beaver moves quickly. It is **diligent** in building and storing food. If its dam has a leak in it, it hurries to repair the break. Beavers use their strong front teeth to cut down trees and to peel off the bark and the branches. The animal gnaws the branches off the tree, then it carries, drags, pulls, pushes, or rolls the log into the water. It stores some branches deep in the water for use as food during the winter. The other branches may be used to enlarge or repair the dam and the lodge—home. The beaver is **diligent** to work alone, or sometimes with others of its kind.

Life requires children to practice character qualities so they may become productive adults. **Diligence** is an important characteristic to have as this is accomplished. So what does it mean to be **diligent**?

1. It just means to steadily apply efforts to accomplish a task.

2. Next it means to exert oneself to fulfill what is undertaken without unnecessary delay.

3. And finally acting with great care and effort.

Diligence is a Latin word meaning "to love earnestly." In other words, whatever work is given you do it with a sincere love for what you do and the purpose for which you do it. The Scriptures tell us: *"Whatsoever ye do, do it heartily, as to the Lord, and not unto men"* (Colossians 3:23).

Three-toed Sloth

Diligent
or
Slothful?

Diligent
or
Slothful?

Diligent
or
Slothful?

Beaver

A **Diligent** Work

"Enlarge the place of thy tent, and let them stretch forth the curtains of thine habitations: spare not, lengthen thy cords, and strengthen thy stakes."

Isaiah 54:2

Mission work is an activity that needs to **diligently** be done for God's kingdom on this Earth. As we study the continents in future lessons, learn about missionaries and their work. We are told: "God's people have a mighty work before them, a work that must continually rise to greater prominence. Our efforts in missionary lines must become far more extensive. A more decided work than has been done must be done prior to the second appearing of our Lord Jesus Christ.

"God's people are not to cease their labors until they shall encircle the world. The vineyard includes the whole world, and every part of it is to be worked. There are places which are now a moral wilderness, and these are to become as the garden of the Lord. The waste places of the Earth are to be cultivated, that they may bud and blossom as the rose. New territories are to be worked by men inspired by the Holy Spirit. New churches must be established, new congregations organized. At this time there should be representatives of present truth in every city, and in the remote parts of the Earth. The whole Earth is to be illuminated with the glory of God's truth. The light is to shine to all lands and all peoples. And it is from those who have received the light that it is to shine forth. The day-star has risen upon us, and we are to flash its light upon the pathway of those in darkness.

"A crisis is right upon us. We must now by the Holy Spirit's power proclaim the great truths for these last days. It will not be long before every one will have heard the warning and made his decision. Then shall the end come. It is the very essence of all right faith to do the right thing at the right time. God is the great Master-Worker, and by His providence He prepares the way for His work to be accomplished."*

God has laid a foundation for this work in past generations. Today is the day to work for the souls of people to prepare them for what is coming upon this Earth. Read the following story about how God used one man in the past who worked **diligently** for Him!

With God At Dawn 30

Count Nicolas Ludwig Zinzendorf

"How often those who trusted the word of God, though in themselves utterly helpless, have withstood the power of the whole world...Such examples are not found in the Bible only. They abound in every record of human progress. The Vaudois and the Huguenots, Wycliffe and Huss, Jerome and Luther, Tyndale and Knox, Zinzendorf and Wesley, with multitudes of others, have witnessed to the power of God's word against human power and policy in support of evil. These are the world's true nobility. This is its royal line. In this line the youth of today are called to take their places."*

Two of the six Eskimo boys sent by Egede to Copenhagen from Greenland were present at the coronation of King Christian VI, in 1731. A young count was also there to represent the Saxon court, who in the excitement of the occasion did not forget that he was an ambassador for a higher court. He learned with sorrow from these boys that the mission in Greenland was to be broken up; and at the same time his attendants heard from Anthony, a native from St. Thomas, West Indies, the sad condition of the slaves in those islands. These stirring tidings sent such a trill of mis-

Education 254-255

sionary impulse to the little church which had been growing up on the estate of this young count, that even now it vibrates in many lands. This count was Zinzendorf, born the opening year of the eighteenth century, the noblest of a long line of nobility. Though not destined to stand at the battle front in missionary conquest, he became one of the most efficient of any in missionary annals in enlisting, inspiring, and preparing recruits.

His father died when Zinzendorf was but a babe; and his mother left him, when a mere child, to the care of his pious grandmother. This godly woman, and an aunt who prayed with him night and morning, led him to the Saviour. To him faith was no guesswork in childhood or in manhood. At the age of four he earnestly sought God, and made this covenant: "Be thou mine, dear Saviour, and I will be Thine." In the ruins of the old castle home where the grandmother lived, only a league from Herrnhut, a window is still shown to visitors, out of which the young boy used to throw letters addressed to the Saviour, telling of his love to Him, in the hope his heavenly Friend would find and read them.

Communion with God, continued through life, kept him from wreck and ruin where so many in places of honor fall, and made him a powerful worker for God. When He was only six years old, as the army of Charles XII of Sweden was in Saxony, a band of soldiers gained entrance to the castle, and finally went into the room in which was the young boy. But they found him praying. He heeded not their presence; for he was in the audience-chamber of One more powerful than they; a holy shield was spread over him. In silence they paused in that royal presence; in silence they withdrew.

He was sent to school at Halle, to be under the care of that earnest home missionary, August Hermann Francke. Amid new surroundings and temptations, the boy, like Joseph in Egypt, was still true to his heavenly Friend. Refusing to be influenced by worldly associates, he at once began to influence others for good; and the first year, when only ten, he formed a young people's society, called "The Order of the Grain of Mustard Seed." Their badge was a shield with the inscription, "His Wounds Our Healing." He had learned by experience that there is a shield for those who flee to those wounds for refuge. The first article of this new order was, "The

members of our society will love the whole human family." They pledged themselves "to confess Christ faithfully, to exercise love toward their neighbors," and "to seek the conversion of others, both Jews and the heathen." Here in spirit was a world's missionary society, a half century before the birth of Carey. Indeed, the Spirit of Christ is a missionary spirit, for neighbors, for Jews, and for the heathen, both nigh and afar off.

In young manhood Zinzendorf wrote, "I would rather be despised and hated for the sake of Jesus than to be beloved for my own sake." And again, "I am as ever, a poor sinner, a captive of eternal love, running by the side of His triumphal chariot, and have no desire to be anything else as long as I live." But a worldly ambitious uncle wished to prepare him for political position, and placed him in the University of Wittenberg, whose walls no longer heard a Martin Luther's voice. But neither secular studies nor university life could overthrow his devotions. Whole days were spent in fasting; entire nights devoted to prayer.

Later he was sent abroad to secure a supposed necessary part of a nobleman's education. The new opportunities for test and wreck of character only revealed more fully the true mettle of the young man. "If the object of my being sent to France is to make me a man of the world," he wrote, "I declare that this money is thrown away; for God will, in His goodness, preserve in me the desire to live only for Jesus Christ."

In the Dusseldorf gallery he saw the wonderfully expressive Ecce Homo painting over which were the words, "This have I done for thee: what hast thou done for Me?" Its effect in deepening his desire to labor for the Master was never lost upon him.

At nineteen he visited the soul-drowning whirlpool, Paris; but he would neither gamble nor dance, at court, nor be drawn by the fashionable follies of the hour. "Good evening, count," said a duchess; "were you at the opera last evening?" "No madam," he replied. "I have no time to go to the opera."

On leaving the wicked city, he exclaimed, as many another has felt to do, "O brilliant misery!"

Although desiring from childhood to enter the ministry, the count yielded to the wishes of his relatives and became a counselor at the court of Dresden. But against their advice, and the known wishes of the king and court, he refused to

attend the fashionable amusements of the city, and he held open his doors for gospel meetings.

At the time of the birth of Zinzendorf it seemed as if Protestantism in intolerant Austria had almost breathed its last. Its adherents had been imprisoned, banished, drowned, and burned. There were a few, however, of the spiritual followers of Wycliffe, Huss, and Jerome, the Moravian brethren, who held to the word of God as their dearest earthly treasure. Here and there was a Bible in a cellar, in a hole in the wall, in a hollow log, or in a space beneath the dog-kennel—a secret which the head of the family would dare to make known, even to his children, only on his death-bed.

But over in Moravia was a young man, Christian David, a Catholic, who never saw a Bible till he was twenty years of age, and down deep in his heart he had a craving which neither prayers to the virgin Mary nor confessions to the parish priest could satisfy. And some one who knew the remedy, dared to place in his hands a copy of the Book of God. In him the living spring was unsealed and its waters gushed forth. Soon other souls, like him, found freedom within, and they longed for freedom without. Very earnestly David sought an asylum for them. At last he was directed to Count Zinzendorf, who, rather than enter into litigation, had given up his paternal inheritance, and purchased a tract of land where was "a perfect wilderness, covered with bushes and trees." On learning from David the condition of his Moravian brethren, the count promised to receive them upon his new estate. Forsaking all, as had the Pilgrims to America, they were secretly led by David to Berthelsdorf; and there, though the count was still in Dresden, a site in the woody wilderness was selected, and building begun. This was in 1722, a little before the marriage of the count. The settlement was called Hernhut, the "Lord's Watch," and here the oppressed from different countries came.

When Zinzendorf married, it was "in the Lord," and to the Noble Countess Dorethea. She, casting "rank and quality to the winds," as he had done, pledged with him, upon the day of their marriage, "to stand ready, at a moment's warning from the Lord, to enter upon mission work, prepared to meet all the obloquy it involved." The countess was not only a missionary in spirit, but like her husband, a composer, and we still sing from her pen:

"O, may Thy knowledge fill the earth!
Increase the number still
Of those who in Thy word believe,
And do Thy holy will."

On their marriage tour they visited Berthelsdorf; and when a home of the refugees was pointed out to him, the count left the carriage, entered, bade them welcome in the name of the Lord, and knelt with them in prayer, commending them to God.

As already related, it was in 1731 that the cry from the islands reached the ears of Zinzendorf. That visit to Copenhagen, says Dr. George Smith, "was the beginning of the Maravian missions." Such a spirit as that of the count could not always be fettered with civil affairs; and he resigned his position at the court, and retired to Hernhut, where was a flock that he regarded as "a parish destined for him from eternity."

The messages of the Eskimos and Nthony were taken up before the congregation. That night a young man, Leonard Dober, could not sleep, he was so deeply impressed with a call to mission work on St. Thomas. What was his surprise and joy to learn, next day, that a young friend of his, Tobias Leupold, was similarly impressed; and what was the still greater surprise of each, on the evening of that day, as with others they passed the door of the count, to hear him say to a visitor, "Sir, among these brethren there are missionaries to the heathen in St. Thomas."

The matter was laid before the congregation, the two young men having expressed a willingness to sell themselves into slavery if need be but to save a single soul. But the church as a whole was not prepared to sanction such evidences of the movings of the Spirit, and it was only after much deliberation and delay that one of the young men, Dober, was permitted to go forth, accompanied by David Nitschmann, with about three dollars apiece for fare and expenses. They left Hernhut to journey six hundred miles to Copenhagen on foot. Zinzendorf took them as far as Bautzen in his carriage, and gave them his parting blessing.

At copenhagen they met fresh opposition and ridicule; but they were not dismayed, and quietly held to their purpose. Their cause at last gained the attention of the royal chaplains and high officials, and finally the queen and Princess Amelia contributed toward their expenses.

They arrived at St. Thomas December 13, 1732. Dober's trials in the home land were only the beginning. Part of the time, he lived on bread and water; but he fed the slaves with bread from heaven. His friend returned to Europe the next spring; and it was sixteen months longer before Dober heard from his Herrnhut home. Suddenly one evening, who should appear before him but Tobias, the friend of his early consecration! He had come as one of a band of eighteen missionaries for this island and St. Croix. Their passage had lasted over half a year; and their stateroom was a pen ten feet by ten, under the second deck, too low for them to sit upright. They suffered much on the way, and some of them died soon after arrival.

Opposition became so strong that the missionaries were thrown into prison. Zinzendorf, not knowing what had taken place, crossed the Atlantic, called at the island, and found his beloved brethren prisoners. He set at work at once for their release, which was accomplished the next day; and the good work went on. It was at this visit that he composed his famous hymn,

"Jesus, Thy blood and righteousness
My beauty are, my glorious dress;
'Mid hosts of sin, in these arrayed,
My soul shall never be afraid."

Dober was willing to lay down his life for one soul. At the end of one hundred years after the establishment of this first Moravian mission, thirteen thousand three hundred and thirty-three persons had been admitted to communion.

Following the example of Dober, the next year, 1733, Christian David went forth to Greenland to answer the call of the two Eskimos, taking with him Matthew and Christian Stach, whom he had led to Hernhut from Catholic persecution in Austria. They were gladly welcomed by Egede. They built a cabin, and called their mission New Hernhut. A beginning had been made by Egede; but the polar bergs are not so frigid as unbelieving hearts, and the sufferings of the missionaries were only fully penned by the angel writers from heaven. It was fourteen years before they could build their first church.

In 1734 Zinzendorf was ordained a minister in the Lutheran Church. "All his property he surrendered to the work," says George Smith in his comprehensive "Short History of Missions," "Not of organizing a sect, but of forming circles of pious souls with the Lutheran Church, as Wesley—learning of him—sought to do in the Church of England."

The same year saw the Moravians beginning mission work for the Indians of New York and Pennsylvania. But such good work could not go on forever without interference. In 1736 the count was unjustly torn from the flock and the refuge he had made for others, and was banished on the chargee of introducing "dangerous novelties in religion." But no complaint escaped his lips. He found shelter in more tolerant Holland. "That place is our proper home," said he, "where we have the greatest opportunity of laboring for our Saviour." He established a school to train missionaries from which they went forth to their Heaven-given work.

Zinzendorf testified even before royalty to the truths he had demonstrated by experience. To a princess of Denmark he said: "Christians are God's people, begotten of His Spirit, obedient to Him, enkindled by His fire; His blood is their glory. Before the majesty of the betrothed of God, kingly crowns grow pale; a hut to them becomes a palace. Sufferings under which heroes would pine, are gladly borne by loving hearts which have grown strong through the cross."

Ten years of banishment, calumny, and slander did not sour him. Three times the government of Saxony investigated the charges made against him. "The devils in hell," was the strong language of King William of Prussia, "could not have fabricated worse lies." He was completely exonerated; and at the request of this same king he was ordained bishop of the Moravians in 1737. In this same year, in response to the appeal Ziegenbalg had sent from South Africa, George Schmidt, "the Bohemian Bunyan," was sent forth to the Hottentots of that land, who until the missionaries went to them, were treated as beasts.

In 1741 Count Zinzendorf visited America, and founded the celebrated Moravian colony at Bethlehem, Pennsylvania. The next year, in company with Spangenberg, who became his successor, he formed the first Indian Moravian Church, at Shekomeco, near where Brainerd began his work a year later.

In 1744 the scarlet thread bound Hernhut to the Indians of South America. Thus the mustard-seed grew, and became as it were a tree, an emblem of the tree of life, whose leaves are for the healing of the nations; and its branches have been traced far enough to teach us that one young person fully consecrated to the Master's service may unseal springs of life that will never cease to flow.

It was the perfect peace, during a terrific storm, possessed by a company of German Moravians, that so impressed John Wesley during his missionary voyage to America in 1736. While the English passengers were screaming with fright, the Moravians calmly sang praise to Him who "make the storm a calm," "and bringeth them unto their desired haven."

"Were you not afraid?" Wesley asked one of them.

"I thank God, no," he replied.

"But were not your women and children afraid?"

"No," he mildly answered; "our women and children are not afraid to die."

The holy shield of trust that had turned back King Charles's soldiers form the boy of six, had protected the singing pilgrims from fear and from the elements.

On returning from America in 1738 Wesley visited Zinzendorf, but seems not to have been so deeply impressed by him as by some of the lesser lights among his followers.

In 1747 the count was permitted to visit Herrnhut, and in 1755 was allowed to return there permanently. When he made the announcement which thrilled the hearts of Dober and Leupold, his congregation numbered six hundred, including women and children. In 1905 the world membership of the Moravian Church was 101,391, and during the one hundred seventy years it had sent out a total of 2,300 missionaries. For half a century after forming the Order of the mustard-Seed, Zinzendorf was spared to scatter and nourish the gospel seed. One hundred works, in prose and verse, poured from his pen. Amidst all the care of increasing missions and organizations, he continued to labor for individual souls. One secret of the success of the Moravian missions is the small outlay—but three per cent, it is said—for executive management.

One of the most remarkable men of modern times, Zinzendorf's experience was in harmony with his words, "The whole world is the Lord's; men's souls are all His; I am debtor to all."*

Nicolas Ludwig Zinzendorf was **diligent** to help in sending the message of Christ into all the Earth.

The Advance Guard of Missions 50

Reinforce
Missions
𝕲o ye therefore, and teach all nations...."
Matthew 28:19

1. What are you doing as a missionary? Find a project you can do with your family:

  • Start with your family;

  • Next go to the neighbors; and

  • Finally reach out beyond your neighborhood.

2. Do you have any returned missionaries in your church? Maybe your mother could invite them to have Sabbath dinner with your family. Ask them questions about their work in the mission field. Find out the needs there. Perhaps, your family could help that mission.

3. Before lunch each day read a continued mission story book.

4. Help with a mission project in your local church.

About the Earth and God's People
"He came unto his own, and his own received him not."
John 1:11

The Earth is a large sphere which is a ball-shaped body. It is covered with water, rocks, and soil and encircled with air. It is one of the planets in our solar system that **diligently** travels through space with the sun. As you know, suns are stars. Our sun is one of the billions of stars that make up the galaxy called the Milky Way. The Milky Way and countless other galaxies make up the universe. As God had a plan in creating the Earth, the solar system, and the universe, so He had a plan for "His Chosen People." He desired them to **diligently** serve and follow Him, the *"Sun of Righteousness,"* even as planet Earth **diligently** follows the sun through the universe. They were not only to follow Him but to encourage others to do the same.

The Earth is hardly a speck in the universe, but God, who created all, came to this Earth to live. In all His big universe His heart of love was especially drawn to the one planet that sinned, and particularly to "His Chosen People," the Hebrews. We are told, "For more than a thousand years the Jewish people had awaited the Saviour's coming. Upon this event they had rested their brightest hopes. In song and prophecy, in temple rite and household prayer, they had enshrined His name. And yet at His coming they knew Him not. The Beloved of heaven was to them *'as a root out of a dry ground,'* He had *'no form nor comeliness;'* and they saw in Him no beauty that they should desire Him. *'He came unto his own, and his own received him not'* (Isaiah 53:2; John 1:11).

Reminder
Diligence

Some synonyms for **diligence** are perseverance, industriousness, persistence, and constancy. We could say this word means stick-to-it-iveness!

"Seest thou a man diligent in his business? he shall stand before kings; he shall not stand before mean men."
Proverbs 22:29

"Yet God had chosen Israel. He had called them to preserve among men the knowledge of His law, and of the symbols and prophecies that pointed to the Saviour. He desired them to be as wells of salvation to the world. What Abraham was in the land of his sojourn, what Joseph was in Egypt, and Daniel in the courts of Babylon, the Hebrew people were to be among the nations. They were to reveal God to men."*

God wanted His chosen ones to respond to those living in the world as He did to people when He lived on Earth. *"But when he saw the multitudes, he was moved with <u>compassion</u> on them, because they fainted, and were scattered abroad, as sheep having no shepherd. Then saith he unto his disciples, the harvest truly is plenteous, but the labourers are few; Pray ye therefore the Lord of the harvest, that he will send forth labourers into his harvest"* (Matthew 9:36-38).

*The Desire of Ages 27

Laborers

"...He will send forth labourers...."

Reinforce
**Read this poem
before reading the next section.**

Belongs

The earth belongeth to the Lord,
And all that it contains;
The world that is inhabited
And all that there remains.
—*C.M.D. Varina*

Just Right

"The earth is the Lord's, and the fulness thereof; the world, and they that dwell therein."

Psalm 24:1

The Earth is just the right distance from the sun for people, animals, and plants to live. They need the sun's warmth and light. If the Earth was too close to the sun it would be too hot for living things. If it was too far away from the sun, it would be too cold for living things. How sad it was that the chosen people had grown spiritually cold because they were not living close enough to *"the Sun of Righteousness."*

Water covers much of the Earth and is needed for all living things. The lesson we can learn from this necessity for an abundance of water is: "He who seeks to quench his thirst at the fountains of this world will drink only to thirst again. Everywhere men are unsatisfied. They long for something to supply the need of the soul. Only One can meet that want. The need of the world, *'The Desire of all nations,'* is Christ [Water of Life]. The divine grace which He alone can impart, is as living water, purifying, refreshing, and invigorating the soul."* It is a never failing, bountiful Source from the Water of Life.

All that man needs to live is provided by God on this Earth—air, water, and food. *"...For all the earth is mine"* (Exodus 19:5). He has provided also for the spiritual needs of His chosen people, today.

The Desire of Ages 187

A thin layer of rock called the crust covers the Earth's surface. All living things live on the crust or in the water covering 70 per cent of the earth. Beneath the Earth's surface is the mantle and cores.

In later lessons in Nature we will study more in detail about the geology of planet Earth.

A thin layer of rock called the crust covers the Earth's surface.

Remarkable Facts
Planet Earth

Age – About six thousand years

Weight – 6.6 sextillion – 6,600,000,000,000,000,000,000 short tons (6.0 sextillion metric tons).

Motion – Rotates once every 23 hours, 56 minutes, 4.09 seconds. Revolves around the sun once every 365 days, 6 hours, 9 minutes, 9.54 seconds.

"If any man thirst, let him come unto me, and drink.

"He that believeth on me, as the Scripture hath said, out of his belly shall flow rivers of living water."
John 7:37-38

Size – Distance from one pole to the other through the Earth – 7,899.83 miles (12,713.54 kilometers). The distance through the Earth at the equator – 7,926.41 miles (12,756.32 kilometers). The distance from one pole to the other over the surface of the Earth – 24,859.82 miles (40,008.00 kilometers).

The distance around the Earth at the equator – 24,901.55 miles (40,075.16 kilometers).

Christopher Columbus believed that one could reach the east by sailing west, but he underestimated the size of the planet. Therefore, when he reached the Caribbean, he thought he was in India and called the natives "Indians." The Earth is more than three times bigger than Columbus first thought!

Area – Total surface area – 196,800,000 square miles (509,700,000 square kilometers). Land area about 57,300,000 square miles (148,400,000 square kilometers). 29 percent of the total surface area. Water area – about 139,500,000 square miles, (361,300,000 square kilometers), which is 71 per cent of total surface area.

Surface – Highest land – Mount Everest, 29,028 feet (8,848 meters) above sea level. Lowest land – shore of Dead Sea, about 1,310 feet (399 meters) below sea level. Deepest part of the ocean – area of the Mariana Trench in Pacific Ocean south west of Guam, 36,198 feet (11,033 meters) below surface.

Draw the country where you live.

Temperature – Highest, 136° F. (58° C.) at Al Aziziyah, Libya. Lowest, -128° F. (-89.6° C.) at Vostok Station in Antarctica. Average surface temperature, 57° F. (14° C.).

Atmosphere – The height of more than 99 per cent of the atmosphere is less than 50 miles (80 kilometers) above the earth's surface. Particles of the atmosphere are 1,000 miles (1,600 kilometers) above the surface. The chemical makeup of the atmosphere is 78 per cent nitrogen, 21 per cent oxygen, 1 per cent argon with small amounts of other gases.

Chemical Makeup – of the Earth's crust – (in per cent of the crust's weight) – oxygen 46.6, silicon 27.7, aluminum 8.1, iron, 5.0, calcium 3.6, sodium 2.8, potassium 2.6, magnesium 2.0, and other elements totaling 1.6 per cent.

Age of the Earth

Reflect

"For six thousand years, faith has builded upon Christ. For six thousand years the floods and tempests of satanic wrath have beaten upon the Rock of our salvation; but it stands unmoved."

—*The Desire of Ages* 413

"For six thousand years that master-mind that once was highest among the angels of God, has been wholly bent to the work of deception and ruin."

—*The Great Controversy* (1888) f.4

"The laws and operations of nature, which have engaged men's study for six thousand years, were opened to their [Adam and Eve] minds by the infinite Framer and Upholder of all."

—*Christian Education* 207

"For six thousand years the great controversy has been in progress; the Son of God and his heavenly messengers have been in conflict with the power of the evil one, to warn, enlighten, and save the children of men."

—*The Great Controversy* 656

"The fact that he [man] has for six thousand years withstood the ever-increasing weight of disease and crime is conclusive proof of the power of endurance with which he was first endowed."

—*Christian Temperance and Bible Hygiene* 71

"The great controversy between Christ and Satan, that has been carried forward for nearly six thousand years, is soon to close; and the wicked one redoubles his efforts to defeat the work of Christ in man's behalf and to fasten souls in his snares."

—*The Great Controversy* 518

"The continual trangression of man for over six thousand years has brought sickness, pain, and death as its fruit. And as we draw near the close of time, Satan's temptations to indulge appetite will be more powerful, and more difficult to resist."

—*Christian Temperance and Bible Hygience* 154

"And many who profess to believe the Bible record are at a loss to account for wonderful things which are found in the earth, with the view that creation week was only seven literal days, and that the world is now only about six thousand years old. These, to free themselves from difficulties thrown in their way by infidel geologists, adopt the view that the six days of creation were six vast, indefinite periods, and the day of God's rest was another indefinite period, making senseless the fourth commandment of God's holy law."
—*I The Spirit of Prophecy* 87

"Those who are destroying the earth have had a long probation. For six thousand years God has borne with the ignorance and wickedness of men. In every possible way He has tested and tried them, seeking to lead them to return to their loyalty, and be saved. But they refuse to listen to His entreaties. War and bloodshed have been, are still, and will continue to be."
—*I Manuscript Releases* 61

"For six thousand years, Satan's work of rebellion has *'made the earth to tremble.'*"
—*The Great Controversy* 659

About 6,000 Years

"During his experience of nearly six thousand years he [Satan] has lost none of his skill and shrewdness."
—*2 Testimonies* 171

"For six thousand years he [Satan] has wrought his will, filling the earth with woe, and causing grief throughout the universe. The whole creation has groaned and travailed together in pain."
—*The Great Controversy* 673

"More than six thousand years of continual practice has greatly increased his skill to deceive and allure. On the other hand, he who once yields to temptation becomes spiritually weak, and yields more readily the second time. Every repetition of sin blinds his eyes, stifles conviction, and weakens his power of resistance. Thus while the power of the human race to resist temptation is continually decreasing, Satan's skill and power to tempt are continually increasing. This is one great reason why the temptations of the last days will be more severe than those of any other age."
—*Historical Sketches* 133

Remarkable Facts
Israel
God's blessing on Israel in the past is still seen today.

• The state of Israel has only .8 percent of the world's population and is the world's 100th smallest country. But has many remarkable accomplishments.

• 24 percent of Israel's workforce hold university degrees; 12 percent hold advanced degrees. That is the highest ratio in the world.

• Israel has the second largest number of startup companies in the world.

• Israel's economy of $100 billion is larger than all of its immediate neighbors combined.

• Israel has the highest average standard of living in the Middle East and also exceeds the United Kingdom.

• Israel produces more scientific papers per capita than any other nation by a large margin—as well as one of the highest per capita rates of patents filed.

• Israel has the world's second highest number of new books per capita.

• Israel has the highest percentage of home computers per capita.

• The cell phone was developed in Israel by Motorola.

• Israel is the only country in the world that entered the 21st century with a net gain in its number of trees.

• With an aerial arsenal of over 250 F - 16s, Israel has the second largest fleet of fighter aircraft.

• Israel developed the airline industry's most impenetrable flight security. U.S. officials now look to Israel for advice on how to handle airborne security threats.

• Relative to its population, Israel is the largest immigrant-absorbing nation on Earth.

• Israel has more museums per capita than any other country in the world.

• In 1991, during the first Gulf War, the Israel Philharmonic Orchestra played a concert wearing gas masks as scud missiles fired by Saddam Hussein fell on Tel Aviv.

Review

Place I - II - III

1. How old is the Earth?

2. Learn to spell Earth, world, and globe. Define these words. Use a dictionary. See the spelling list in the Teacher Section for the rest of your spelling words.

3. What is the work of God's people to be in the world?

4. Orally describe the planet Earth to your teacher or draw a picture.

5. Now tell your teacher all you can remember about the chosen people, Israel, from your Bible lesson.

6. What does **diligence** mean? What does slothfulness mean?

Place II - III

7. Do more research about Sloths and Beavers. Write a report.

8. Write a book report about Count Zinzendorf.

Remind

1. As you are picking up plates to set the table or putting around fruit on the table, remember the shape of the earth (round). God has a plan for it and you. Are you **diligent** to fulfil God's plan?

2. While helping mother make dinner rolls—make them in a round shape.

3. Cookies taste best when baked just right. God created the Earth to get just the right amount of light and heat.

Illustration
Sun, Earth, and Moon

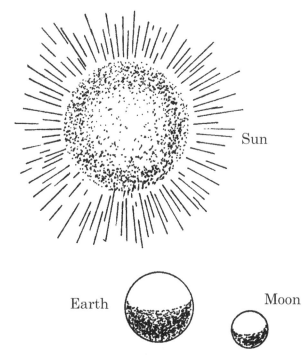

Sun

Earth

Moon

Research
Planet Earth—Size, Distance, Place, and Atmosphere

"And five of them were wise, and five were foolish."
Matthew 25:2

Diameter is the distance through the center of an object. The Earth is the <u>fifth</u> in size as compared to the other planets. Its diameter is about 8,000 miles (13,000 kilometers). The largest planet is about 11 times bigger in diameter than the Earth. The smallest planet is Pluto about one-<u>fifth</u> the size of the Earth's diameter. The chosen people on Earth (<u>5th</u> planet in size) are like the <u>5</u> foolish virgins who had no oil in their lamps (Matthew 25:1-13). Those who claimed to be God's chosen people were not led by the Holy Spirit (oil) but by another spirit—Satan.

Five in the Bible means grace and favor.

The Earth is about 93 million miles (150 million kilometers) from the sun. The two planets that are closer are Mercury and Venus. It is believed their surface is very hot, maybe up to 600° to 800° F. (316° to 427° C.). The Earth's average surface temperature is 57° F. (14° C.). All the other planets except Mars are very cold.

The Earth is the third planet from the sun and the seventh from Pluto.

For a planet to have life like we have on the Earth, it would need oxygen. Air reminds us of the Holy Spirit that God's people need who **diligently** follow Him. They then are like the 5 wise virgins. *"The wind bloweth where it listeth, and thou hearest the sound thereof, but canst not tell whence it cometh, and whither it goeth: so is every one that is born of the Spirit"* (John 3:8). "Christ uses the wind as a symbol of the Spirit of God. As the wind bloweth whither it listeth, and we cannot tell whence it cometh or whither it goeth, so it is with the Spirit of God. We do not know through whom it will be manifested."* Are you a wise or a foolish virgin?

Five Wise Virgins

*II Selected Messages 15

Planet Earth—Held in Place and Movements

"Fear thou not; for I am with thee: be not dismayed;
for I am thy God: I will strengthen thee; yea, I will help thee;
yea, I will __uphold thee__ with the right hand of my righteousness."
Isaiah 41:10

The Earth is so placed in space that it remains as stable as if it were a fixture. The several motions of our planet are carried on so noiselessly and evenly that, as far as we are concerned, all things are as permanent and peaceful as if the old notion of its resting upon pillars were literally true. With what delicacy has the great Artist poised our globe and upheld it ! What power must there be in that hand which has caused so vast a body to know its orbits, and to move so smoothly in it! What engineer can save every part of his machinery from an occasional jar, jerk, or friction? Yet to our great world in its complicated motions no such thing has ever occurred. *"O Lord, my God, thou art very great"* (Psalm 104:1).

As we consider the works of His hand we can so do our work that it will have similar results. Remember, as it is said, *"And whatsoever ye do, do it heartily, as to the Lord, and not unto men"* (Colossians 3:23). Be **diligent** in all that you

---

O Lord, How Manifold Are Thy Works

Let God rejoice in all His works,
And let His works proclaim
Forevermore their Maker's praise
And glorify His name.

---

do! The conviction that one is led by God is a most powerful incentive to doing a task and doing it well! "Let those who are naturally slow of __movement__ seek to become active, quick, energetic, remembering the words of the apostle, *'Not slothful in business; fervent in spirit; serving the Lord.'*

"If it falls to your lot to prepare the meals, make careful calculations, and give yourself all the time necessary to prepare the food, and set it on the table in good order, and on exact time. To have the meal

---

"God's Mercy and love for the fallen race have not ceased to accumulate, nor lost their earthward direction."*

My Life Today 292

ready five minutes earlier than the time you have set is more commendable than to have it five minutes later. But if you are under the control of slow, dilatory <u>movements</u>, if your habits are of a lazy order, you will make a long job out of a short one; and it is the duty of those who are slow to reform and to become more expeditious. If they will, they can overcome their fussy, lingering habits. In washing dishes they may be careful and at the same time do quick work. Exercise the will to this end, and the hands will move with dispatch."* Do not think you cannot overcome a bad habit for God says, *"Fear thou not for I am with thee: be not dismayed; for I am thy God: I will strengthen thee; yea, I will help thee; yea, I will uphold thee with the right hand of my righteousness"* (Isaiah 41:10).

As God has cared for the Earth He "has always had a care for His people...Christ taught His disciples that the amount of divine attention given to any object is proportionate to the rank assigned to it in the creation of God. He called their attention to the birds of the air. Not a sparrow, He said, falls to the ground without the notice of our heavenly Father. And if the little sparrow is regarded by Him, surely the souls of those for whom Christ has died are precious in His sight. The value of man, the estimate God

places upon him, is revealed in the cross of Calvary...."** He even cares for the Earth's movements.

The Earth is always in motion. It has three movements:

(1) Spins like a top spins;
(2) travels around the sun; and
(3) moves through the Milky Way as does the rest of the solar system.

The Earth spins on its axis while it travels around the sun. The axis is the invisible line that connects the North and South poles.

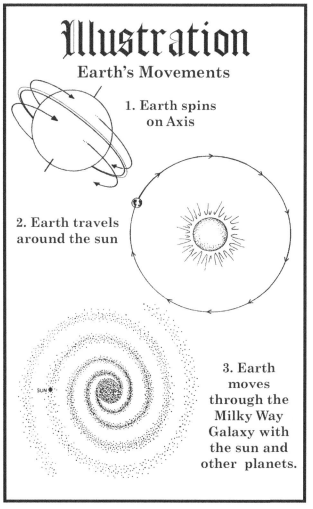

Illustration
Earth's Movements

1. Earth spins on Axis

2. Earth travels around the sun

3. Earth moves through the Milky Way Galaxy with the sun and other planets.

*Child Guidance 125 **My Life Today 292

This motion of the Earth helps us measure the length of days and years. The spinning of the Earth makes the sun look like it is moving from the east to the west, and gives the day and night. Each time the Earth turns once it takes 23 hours, 56 minutes and 4.09 seconds. The daytime is when the Earth is facing the sun, and nighttime is when the Earth faces away from the sun. The sun appears to rise in the east and set in the west. The Earth makes its journey of 595 million miles (959 million kilometers) around the sun every 365 days, 6 hours, 9 minutes, and 9.54 seconds each year. The Earth is traveling at a speed of 66,600 miles (107,200 kilometers) an hour.

The path the Earth travels around the sun is called its orbit. The tilt of the Earth and its trip around the sun causes the change of seasons.

Notice how all the planets, suns, and moons, revolve around something. Examples would be a moon around a planet, a planet around a sun, a solar system around the center of a galaxy, and all moving around the throne of God, the very center of the universe. This can remind us how God wants us to have Him be the center of our lives. His chosen people had been called to this purpose. Were they **diligent**? Yes! In laws and rules but not in the work of the heart.

The Milky Way galaxy spins around like a giant wheel. Our solar system is about three-fifths (3/5) from the center of the edge of the galaxy. The speed at which it moves around the center of the galaxy is 155 miles (250 kilometers) per second. It is thought that it takes our solar system 250 million years to make one trip around the center of the solar system. It has not yet made one full trip.

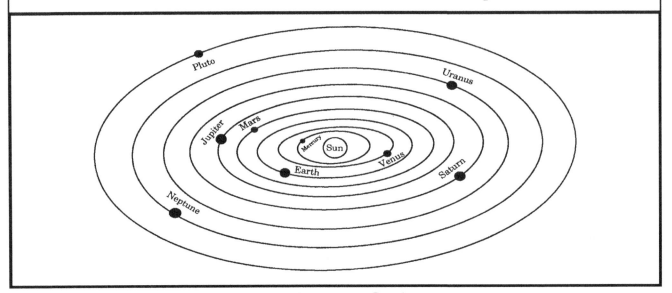

Missions

For I know their works and their thoughts:
it shall come, that I will gather all nations and tongues;
and they shall come, and see my glory.
Isaiah 66:18

It is said that when Columbus set foot upon a border isle of the new world, he fell upon his knees, and with tears of joy, kissed the ground, and thanked God for His great goodness in bringing him safe to land. His comrades, bearing banners of the cross, knelt and wept beside him. The natives collected around him in silent astonishment, while his crew, who had plotted his destruction, threw themselves at his feet and begged his forgiveness. Drawing his sword, he planted the royal standard, and in memory of mercies his God had given, called the place "Holy Saviour."

The fact that Columbus was thrown into chains and died in poverty, is only an evidence of the darkness that then covered the earth, and makes his heroism shine out all the brighter. And was not his success a birth-cry of "a new order of things?"—Not a statue of Liberty, but her genius, which cannot be fettered by felons' chains, nor bound behind prison bars? Was not this a touch of her torch, to lighten, not the new land alone, but the world? And was not the hard battle fought out lonehanded by Columbus, which meant so much for the world's future, very like many another, waged by lone soldiers of the cross? Who can doubt that the God Columbus thanked had helped him, or that the cross, then blindly followed, would shed its light over all the land?

Close upon the footsteps of this and other discoveries came the great Reformation in Europe. The word of God was unchained from convent walls; the cross brought down from church steeples and planted in human hearts. Then there followed a tide of worldliness and formalism. The streams that make glad the city of God seemed confined, on earth, to tiny rills. But God keeps watch above His own. Of this little world that received the life-blood of His Son, He is ever mindful, as of the one lost sheep.

To trace some of these refreshing rills of influence, to survey a few of the battlefield of individual victory, hoping thus to aid the reader in his own deep struggles and help to prepare him for final triumph....

As the writer has looked upon the drama, not of moving but of living pictures, and beheld such transformations of character as would cause the angels to wonder and rejoice, there has fallen upon his soul the hope that this may prove one more bugle-call for recruits to join in similar warfare. When lips once stained with oaths and lying have been touched with fire from heaven's altar and trusted with the gospel story, when minds once the devil's workshop have become fitted to deal with the souls of men, when hearts oft defiled with hate and murder have become channels for the love of Christ, can there be stronger evidence that similar victories may still be gained and volunteers enlisted in God's loyal army!....

—*C. G. Howell*

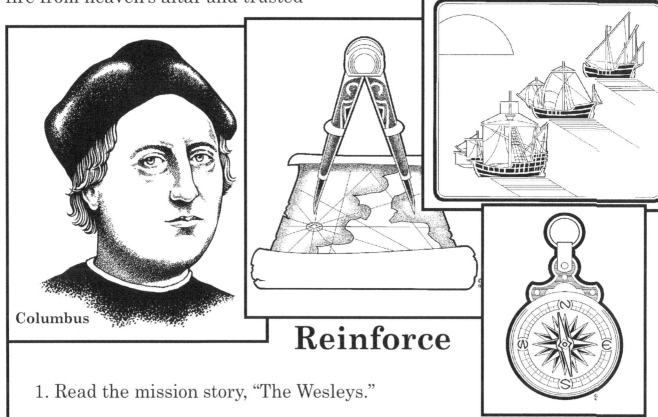

Columbus

Reinforce

1. Read the mission story, "The Wesleys."

2. Do the experiment about the movement of the Earth on the next page.

3. Search for fives in nature.

4. As a family, help one another have more efficient movements in work habits.

Reinforce
Experiment – Motion of the Earth

Materials Needed: 1 square piece of cardboard 4" x 4" (10 cm x 10cm)
Clock
Scissors
Tape
Several pieces of paper
Pencil

Step 1 – Choose a sunny day to do this experiment.

Step 2 – Cut a one-inch (2 cm) hole in the center of a cardboard square.

Step 3 – Find a south-facing window that receives full sun.

Step 4 – Tape the square piece on cardboard on the window so the sun will shine through the hole onto the floor.

Step 5 – Place one piece of paper where the sun hits it.

Step 6 – Check the floor every 30 minutes. Each time place another piece of paper on the floor.

Explanation: The spot of light moves from left to right and change its position as the day continues. Why? Because the Earth rotates from west to east every 24 hours while it travels around the sun. This movement of the Earth causes the spot of sunlight to move across one paper to the next as this world moves from sunrise to sunset.

If but to perpetuate the memory of Susanna Wesley and give some ideas of her methods of training her children, the illustration in the life of her son John should be given. She looked upon children as a trust committed to parents by the Lord to be trained for Him.

John Wesley, the founder of the Methodist Church, was born at Epworth, England, June 17, 1703. He was the fifteenth of nineteen children. Only ten of these, however, lived to maturity. They lived in the midst of deep poverty, with rural surroundings the most crude and uninviting; but for two centuries her example has been declaring that it is possible, under most untoward circumstances, to train children on this earth for the kingdom of heaven. So highly did John Wesley esteem his mother's methods that after he had grown to manhood he asked her to write them out.

"It can not be of any service to any one," was her underestimate, "to know how I, that have lived such a retired life for so many years, used to employ my time and care in bringing up my children. No one can, without renouncing the world in the most literal sense, observe my method. There are few, if any, that would entirely devote twenty years of the prime of life in hopes to save the souls of their children, which they think may be saved without so much ado; for that was my principal intention, however unskillfully managed."

First and foremost, the will of the child must be subject to the parent's control, "because," said she, and truly too, "this is the only strong and rational foundation of a religious education, without which both precept and example will be ineffectual." So thoroughly was this accomplished with her children, that "there was no difficulty in making them take the most unpleasant medicine."

It was a rule, not to be modified in any case, that no child was to have anything it cried for. "The moral effect on the child's mind," observes Dr. Fitchett, "of the discovery that the one infallible way of not getting a desirable thing was to cry for it, must have been surprising." Likewise it was useless to expect a permission once denied, to be granted because a thing was teased for.

The children were carefully trained to be quiet at family prayers; and this was the secret of good behavior in the house of God. They early learned to distinguish the day of worship from other days of the week.

Mrs. Wesley believed the Scripture teaching that the rod furnishes a valuable means of discipline; and before her babes were a year old, they were taught to fear it. The giving way to uncontrolled fits of anger was not allowed. If a child cried, it must "cry softly."

At the age of five they were taught their letters. Reading came next, beginning with Genesis 1:1. "Sukey," said Samuel Wesley to the mother one day, "I wonder at your patience. You have told that child twenty times the same thing."

"Had I satisfied myself with mentioning the matter only nineteen," replied the mother-teacher, "I should have lost all my labor. You see it was the twentieth time that crowned the whole."

An hour each evening was set apart for religious conversation, instruction, Bible study, and prayer, alone with one of the children. John's hour came on Thursday evening. As the older ones grew in experience, they were placed as instructors of the younger ones, reading the Bible and praying together.

Epworth was not the most favorable place for training children. It was a market-town, in a region little better then a swamp. The inhabitants were "perhaps as ignorant and brutal a set of half-heathen as could have been found in England." They disliked the rector's polities, "vexed and harassed him, burned his crops, and hocked his cattle, and finally burned down his rectory."

This incident occurred when John was about five years old. All the other members of the family had escaped from the flaming building. Little John found himself shut up in an upstairs room, the stairs all aflame. The father lost hope, and was praying in an agony of despair. Just before the roof fell in, a man climbed upon the shoulders of another, and grasped the child through the window, and all three escaped. The father called the assembled people to bow with him and thank God for the rescue of his child; and Mrs. Wesley felt that this son had been spared to do a special work for God. After Wesley launched forth in his career as a minister, he often looked back upon this narrow escape, feeling that he was indeed "a brand plucked from the burning." "The incident became a mystic picture of the condition of the whole world, and of the part he was to play in it. His theology translated itself into the terms of that night scene. The burning house was a symbol of a perishing world."

When John was about nine years old, another forcible parable of his life-work was enacted in his humble home. The father was away attending convocation. Mrs. Wesley held her convocation in her kitchen. She began some meetings for her children and servants; and soon some others came in. A report of the informal meetings got to the ears of the very formal churchman, the elder Wesley; and he remonstrated with his good Susanna. For one thing it "looked particular."

"I grant it does," replied the thoughtful matron, "and so does almost anything that is serious, or that may in any way advance the glory of God or the salvation of souls, if it be performed out of a pulpit."

He deemed it unsuitable to her sex; to which Mrs. Wesley replied: "As I am a woman, so I am also mistress of a large family; and though the superior charge of the souls contained in it lies upon you as head of the family, and as their minister, yet in your absence I can not but look upon every soul you leave under my care as a talent committed to me under a trust by the great Lord of all the families of heaven and earth. And if I am unfaithful to Him or to you, how shall I answer when He shall command me to render an account of my stewardship?" She then closes her defense with words so dignified, so terrible in their depth of meaning, that even the stern Samuel Wesley yielded the battle: "If you do, after all, think fit to dissolve this assembly, do not tell me that you desire me to do this; for that will not satisfy my conscience; but send me your positive command, in such full and express terms as may absolve me from guilt and punishment for neglecting this opportunity for doing good, when you and I shall appear before the great and awful tribunal of our Lord Jesus Christ."

The little meetings continued till the rector's return, and lifted the church from a state of apathy to an attendance of hundreds, and an interest before unknown. Some have thought that Methodism began in a student movement at Oxford. Be that as it may, it had a wonderful precedent in Mrs. Wesley's kitchen. God often goes to some unlooked-for place His wonders to perform. It may be but to put a babe in a basket of bulrushes, a mother and child in a stall; and though the earth moves on in its course, quite unconscious, Heaven stoops to speak to it through the cloudy pillar, to illumine its hills with an unknown star, and to waft to its unwilling ears a song from the angelic choirs.

Not long after these meetings John Wesley was sent from home to the public boarding-school at Charterhouse. Here he spent several years. Having his meat stolen by the older boys, to the betterment of his health, he lived principally upon bread.

During his absence from home, what is known as "the Epworth noises" took place. "Who does not know the story of 'Old Jeffrey,'" says one of the latest authorities on Wesley, "has missed one of the best attested and most curious ghost stories in literature....From December 1716, to April, 1717, the rectory was made hideously vocal with mysterious noises, raps on the doors and walls, thumps beneath the floor, the smash of broken crock-ery, the rattle of iron chains, the jingle of falling coins, the tread of mysterious feet. The noises baffled all more prosaic explanations, and were at last assigned by common consent to some restless spirit. They became a sound so familiar that they ceased to be annoying, and the lively girls of the parsonage labeled the unseen but too audible sprite 'Old Jeffrey.'

"The story is told in letters in amplest detail, and by every member of the family in turn, and all the tales were collected by John Wesley himself...and published in the *Arminian Magazine.* There is an element of humor in the varying tones in which the marvelous tale is recited. The rector tells it with masculine directness, and a belief in the ghost which plainly breeds, not fear, but only anger, and a desire to come to close quarters with it, and even to thump it. Mrs. Wesley tells the story, after her practical fashion, with Defoe-like simplicity; the quick-witted girls tell the tale with touches of girlish imagination and humor; a neighboring clergyman, who was called in to assist in suppressing the ghost adds his heavy voice to the churus. The evidence, if it were given in a court of law, and in a trial for murder, would suffice to hang any man."*

Wesley and His Century – Fitchett

Mrs. Wesley's quiet hour, from five to six, on her request, was respected by the ghost; likewise her seasons of sacred devotion. He did not give equal consideration, however, to the stern lector, especially when he prayed for King George I. At such times the sprite would kick against floors and walls most vigorously, and it is said he even pushed the unterrified man. Upon such demonstrations the loyal ector observed, "Were I the king myself, I should rather Old Nick should be my enemy than my friend."

One night when the knockings were especially violent in a certain room, Mr. Wesley and his daughter Nancy entered, and he adjured the spirit to speak. Its only response was to knock. "These spirits love darkness," he said. "Put out the candle, and perhaps it will speak." Nancy put out the candle, but still the knockings continued. "Two Christians are an overmatch for the devil," he said; "go downstairs. It may be when I am alone he will have courage to speak." But he would not speak.

When the demonstration began, the sleeping children would tremble in agitation and fear, which so aroused the father's indignation that he challenged the ghost to meet him in his study, and strided to the door, only to find it firmly held against him.

That these manifestations were supernatural, all the Wesleys believed, and with sufficient cause. That there are two spiritual, supernatural realms, in one of which are "spirits of darkness," in the other spirits of light—"ministering spirits"—the Scriptures plainly declare. It is evident Samuel Wesley believed that these manifestations came from the spirits of darkness; and this is the solution of the whole vexed question. Witness such Scriptures as Isaiah 8:19-20; Revelation 16:14.

So much attention need not have been given these phenomena, but for the more modern manifestations, in myriad forms, in almost every city, where hypnotists, clairvoyants, and Spiritualistic mediums carry on their operations. These spirits of darkness appear to human beings to destroy faith in, and lead away from, the word of God. Instead of yielding to their unholy influence, vainly seeking wisdom from it, or making merchandise of it, the Wesleys held firm to the hand of God and the truths of His word; and instead of their home becoming the cradle of modern Spiritualism, it rather became the nursery of Methodism and the great doctrine of justification by faith. True, the Wesley brothers, John and Charles, sought long and earnestly, in that darkened age, before the light of that blessed doctrine dawned upon them; but when they found it, they fostered it.

From Charterhouse the boys were sent to Oxford. In 1725 John graduated here, and was made fellow of Lincoln College the next year. A year or two later, he entered the priesthood of the Episcopal Church of England, and for some time assisted in the parish of his father at Epworth.

A very noticeable difference between those who have been very useful in the world and those who have not, is that the first discover, even in small circumstances, those principles which reach out into eternity, and seize upon them. These lead to great results. John Wesley's greatness was not due so much to what he originated, as to what he discerned and appropriated.

After he had been in the ministry over fifty years he thus wrote of his brother Charles: "In the year 1725 a young student at Oxford was much affected by reading Kempis's 'Christian Pattern,' and Bishop Taylor's 'Rules of Holy Liv-

ing and Dying.' He found an earnest desire to live according to those rules, and to flee from the wrath to come. He sought for some who would be his companions in the way, but could find none, so that for several years he was constrained to travel alone, having no man either to guide or to help him. But in the year 1729, he found one who had the same desire. They then endeavored to help each other, and in the close of the year were joined by two more." John was one of these. With fasting and prayer they studied together the Christian's Guide-Book, wherein is the assurance, *"Seek, and ye shall find."* One of their number, Mr. Morgan, found so much, that he went forth to tell others, even visiting the prisoners in the castle; and he urged John and Charles to join him. "This he did so frequently," wrote John, "that on the 24th of August, 1730, my brother and I accompanied him." Desiring to be in the right, John wrote his father, inquiring "whether we should now stand still or go forward." That venerable man of seventy replied: "You have reason to bless God, as I do, that you have so fast a friend as Mr. Morgan, who I see in the most difficult service is ready to break the ice for you...Go then, in God's name, in the path to which your Saviour has directed you."

It is well that he received such encouragement, for "ridicule which increased fast" fell upon them. Other members joined them, however, including John Clayton and George Whitefield, the latter "a poor servitor of Pembroke," whose preaching was to become as popular as did that of Wesley. By 1735 their little band had increased to fourteen. So carefully were they to walk according to the rules they thought necessary for holy living, they were nicknamed "Methodists."

For a time Wesley was much concerned over the question of the Sabbath. "Among the Oxford Methodists," says Overton "one of the least known, but one who exercised by far the deepest and most permanent influence over John Wesley, was John Clayton....The subject is so important in connection with John Wesley's mental history, that some extracts from Clayton's letters may be justly inserted. In July, 1733, he writes: 'As to your question about Saturday, I can only answer it by giving an account of how I spend it. I do not look upon it as a preparation for Sunday, but as a festival of itself; and therefore I have continued festival prayer for the three primitive hours, and for morning and evening....I look upon Friday as my preparation for the celebration of the Sabbath [that is, of course, Saturday] and the Lord's day.'"*

Life of John Wesley – Overton

One member of that little group, Mr. Gambold, gives one secret of Wesley's success: "He was blessed with such activity as to be always gaining ground, and such steadiness that he lost none." This same Mr. Gambold was one of the Oxford students in whose welfare Mrs. Wesley took much interest, and whose confession was that he "hardly ever submitted to his [Wesley's] advice at the time he gave it.' The ardent young minister's treatment of the obdurate young student, however, is almost as remarkable as was Mrs. Wesley's of her children. He went right to the student's room, and spent an entire week with him. "He accosted me," says the tardy learner, "with the utmost softness; condoled with me the encumbrances of my constitution; heard all that I had to say; endeavored to pick out my meaning; and yielded to me as far as he could." Thus he treated a proud but tempted young man, who otherwise might have been lost. "It was indeed his custom to humble himself most before the proud; not to reproach them, but in a way of secret intercession, to procure their pardon."

Through a friend Wesley was introduced to James Oglethorpe, who invited him to go to Georgisa to preach to his colonists and the Indians. The idea of becoming a missionary to the Indians took great hold upon him. But it was a step that meant much. He earnestly sought advice, and finally laid the matter before his mother, who said, "Had I twenty sons, I should rejoice that they were all so employed, though I should never see them more." Such was her missionary spirit.

It was in 1736 that Wesley came to America. With untiring energy he threw himself into his duties at Savannah. The Indians were then so full of fight, and of doubt as to the value of the religion of the whites, that Oglethorpe advised him to labor for the colonists. Some of the time he held as high as six services in one day. He gathered the children into a school. When the well-to-do children made fun of the barefooted pupils, Wesley took the teacher's place, and went barefooted himself for a week. Thus the students were cured of their impropriety. He fasted twice a week; and when he did eat, he lived mostly on bread and fruit, and through storm and heat bore his most wearing labor without complaint.

Wesley's ministrations in Georgia were not received by all with favor. He had not yet burst through the fetters of formalism that bound him; and an unhappy love affair was turned to injure his influence and to return him, sad at heart, to England. Many have the idea that his work in America was a failure; but his successor George Whitefield, speaks of it thus: "What the good John Wesley has done in America is inexpressible....He has laid a foundation that I hope neither men nor devils will ever be able to shake."

Under a cloud of discouragement and self-censure, however, he returned to his native land, arriving early in 1738. Here he providentially met the Moravian Peter Bohler, to whom he afterward attributed his emergence from the bondage of doubt. Wesley questioned if he would not quit preaching till he had that faith and love which cast out fear and doubt. Here Bohler's advice was of great value: "Preach faith till you have it. And then because you have it, you will preach faith."

The varied fluctuations of his spiritual state, from the time he felt his heart "strangely warmed" on hearing Luther's comments read, until he learned not to depend upon a happy flight of feeling for assurance, need not be traced. From the shifting shades of emotion, to the promises made sure to the obedient, he was lifted where feeling was not mistaken for faith. There is no evidence that the faith which enabled its Possessor to rebuke the winds, and to say to the sea, "Peace, be still," was at that moment thrilling Him with ecstasy; nor did the gloom of the night of His betrayal prevent His inspiring command, "Be of good cheer."

After the heroic Wesley, to make his confidence more strong in the new, had journeyed on foot to Zinzendorf, in banishment at Marienborn, and thence 350 miles to Herrnhut itself, he returned to England to undertake that wonderful campaign of which a perishing people were so much in need. He had been profoundly impressed with the Moravian community. "God has given me at length," he wrote while there, "the desire of my heart. I am with a church whose conversation is in heaven." On meeting Peter Bohler again in England, he wrote: "I marvel how I refrain from joining these men. I scarce can ever see any of them but my heart burns with me." But had he done so, how could he have so moved the Church of England which he so longed to reform?

That he finally became happily wedded to his work none will deny. If he had been as happily married to some genial woman, every sympathetic friend would be glad. A singularly sad story, too long and intricate for detail, is connected with his several love affairs. He was a man of a tender heart; and God made the human heart for human love. Let it be said that at forty-eight, he was married, hastily—"in the Lord," he believed, but the event proved far otherwise. We fain would lift our heroes into the realm where mistakes are never made; but intimate acquaintance with humanity, and some acquaintance with God, leads one to wonder more and more that He unites Himself, through His Son, with such erring mortals as human beings are.

As Charles had been first to enter a deeper experience, and Morgan to lead out in labors for the unfortunate, so Whitefield was first to enter the sphere in which John Wesley's greatest successes were won—that of field preaching. Whitefield made but a short stay in Georgia; but on his return, finding the churches closed against him, he went to the "ignorant, lewd, profane, and brutal" colliers, "the terror of the law and the despair of philanthropy." At his first meeting he had about one hundred listeners; at his fifth, ten thousand. And when Wesley was shut out of the churches, he too, after a struggle with himself, began open-air meetings. "More and more," he said, his hearers "were cut to the heart, and came to me all in tears, inquiring, with the utmost eagerness, what they must do to be saved. I said, 'If all of you will meet on Thursday evening, I will advise you as well as I can.' The first evening, about twelve persons came; the next week, thirty or forty. When they were increased to about a hundred, I took down their names and places of abode, intending, as often as it was convenient, to call upon them at their own houses. Thus, without any previous plan or design, began the Methodist society in England, a company of people associating together to help each other to work out their own salvation.

"The next spring we were invited to Bristol and Kingswood, where likewise societies were quickly formed....Such was the rise and such was the progress of Methodism, from the beginning to the present time (1787). But you will naturally ask, What is Methodism?...Methodism, so-called, is the old religion, the religion of the Bible, the religion of the primitive church...the loving God with all our heart, and soul, and strength, as having first loved us...and the loving every soul which God hath made, every man on earth, as our own soul."

Such was Wesley's definition of Methodism. Let it here be observed that however faultless the form of doctrine, it can only be made impressive upon others for good, to the extent it is lived by its teacher. So closely did Wesley follow the steps of his Master, that even while the common people heard him gladly, the enemy stirred the rude rabble to break up his work. Violence was often shown him; he was struck and dragged; drawn before magistrates, execrated, maligned. But God suffered them not to do him great harm. A mighty work he had to do and he did it for Him.

Of the social conditions at the time, Professor Winchester remarks: "The concurrent testimony of history and literature forces us to believe that never before had what called itself the best society in England shown less refinement, intelligence, or purity than just at the moment when John Wesley began his work." Vital godliness was about as near its death-swoon as at any time following the Reformation. It is stated that every sixth shop in London was a gin-shop.

It was far from Wesley to think of forming a new church. The idea of "societies" within the church was of long standing; and it was his design by such means to quicken the life of the English Church. But anything like enthusiasm, even in saving souls, was not to be tolerated in the church. Like the meetings in Mrs. Wesley's kitchen, it "appeared singular." Even Bishop Butler, whose "Analogy" had just been published, said to Wesley; "Sir, since you ask my advice, I will give it freely—you have no business here; you are not commissioned to preach in this diocese. I therefore advise you to not hence."

The earnest little clergyman replied: "My lord, my business on earth is to do what good I can. Wherever, therefore, I think I can do most good, there must I stay so long as I think so. At present I think I can do most good here; therefore here I stay." In later years, when the keen edge of his sword was somewhat softened, it is probable he would have replied to the good bishop of Bristol somewhat more gently; but the accusation of proselyting dismayed him not.

To another who had charged him with meddling "with souls that did not belong to him," he replied: "God in Scripture commands me according to my power to instruct the ignorant, reform the wicked, confirm the virtuous. Man forbids me to do this in another's parish— that is, in effect, to do it at all; seeing I have now no parish of my own nor probably ever shall. Whom, then, shall I hear—God or man?...I look upon the world as my parish; thus far I mean that in whatever

part of it I am, I judge it meet, right, and my bounden duty to declare unto all that are willing to hear the glad tidings of salvation."*

On returning to the home scenes at Epworth, he desired once more to enter the pulpit which his father had held so long, but the privilege was denied him. But there was one spot on earth which neither Bishop Butler nor the curate of Epworth could well deny the devoted Wesley, and that was his father's tomb. Mounting the sacred mound, hallowed by the memories of the dead, and with the burden of human souls resting upon him, John Wesley, with lips touched with holy fire, spoke as standing between the living and the dead, and summoned his hearers to behold the great purpose of their existence— that they might love and serve God in this life and have life eternal. Immense crowds gathered as he stood on that solemn spot and lifted their minds to eternal themes. A great awakening followed this singular series of sermons.

An illustration of Wesley's sermons may be given from his sermons on the law: " *Think not that I am come to destroy the law, or the prophets: I am not come to destroy, but to fulfil'* The ritual or ceremonial law, delivered by Moses to the children of Israel, containing

Life of John Wesley – Winchester

all the injunctions and ordinances which related to the old sacrifices and service of the temple, our Lord did indeed come to destroy, to dissolve, and utterly abolish...But the moral law contained in the Ten Commandments, and enforced by the prophets, He did not take away. It was not the design of His coming, to revoke any part of this. This is a law which never can be broken, which *stands fast as the faithful witness in heaven.'*...This was from the beginning of the world, being *'written not on tables of stone,'* but on the hearts of all the children of men, when they came out of the hands of the Creator. And however the letters once written by the finger of God are now in a great measure defaced by sin, yet they can not wholly be blotted out, while we have any consciousness of good and evil. Every part of this law must remain in force upon all mankind, and in all ages, as not depending either on time or place, or any other circumstances liable to change, but on the nature of God, and the nature of man, and their unchangeable relation to each other.

"There is, therefore, the closest connection that can be conceived, between the law and the gospel. On the one hand the law continually makes way for and points us to the gospel; on the other, the gospel continually leads us to a exact fulfilling of the law."*

"This law...is the face of God unveiled. It prescribes exactly what is right. By this the sinner is discovered to himself. To slay the sinner is the first use of the law; to destroy the life and strength wherein he trusts. I can not spare the law one moment, no more than I can spare Christ, seeing I now want it as much to keep me to Christ as I ever wanted it to bring me to Him. Each is continually sending me to the other—the law to Christ, and Christ to the law. The love of God in Christ endears the law to me."**

For long years the voice of rebuke to pride was heard by Wesley's followers. When he saw some slipping away from early simplicity, he spared not. "O, ye pretty triflers," were his words in 1787, "I entreat you not to do the devil's work any longer....Let me see, before I die, a Methodist congregation full as plainly dressed as a Quaker congregation. Let your dress be cheap as well as plain; otherwise you do trifle with God and man, and your own souls. No *Quaker linen*; no Brussels lace; no elephantine hats or bonnets—those scandals of female modesty."

*Sermons, Volume 1, 221-223 – Wesley **Sermon 34

For many years Wesley traveled on horseback rising at four o'clock, and usually holding a meeting at five, then away to another appointment. His habit of early rising was formed on this wise: On losing some sleep, he secured an alarm to wake him at seven. He lost sleep the next night; then he set his alarm for six. Still losing sleep, he set it for five. Not sleeping the entire night, he set the alarm for four o'clock. Then no sleep was lost; and for sixty years four o'clock was his rising hour. He came to believe that too much sleep inebriates.

After he began his open-air preaching, he is said to have traveled 225,000 miles, mostly on horseback; preached over 41,000 sermons; published about 200 volumes; and gave away $150,000. One of his favorite maxims was, "always in haste; never in a hurry."

Three years before his death, he wrote: "I went over to Kingswood. Sweet recess, where everything is just as I wish! But—
'Man was not born in shades to lie.
Let us work now; we shall rest by
and by!' "

The text of his last sermon was, *"Seek ye the Lord while he may be found, call ye upon him while he is near."* His last letter, a little before he died, was to William Wilberforce. "Go on," he bade him, in his crusade against human slavery, "in the name of God and the power of His might."

John Wesley died in London, England, March 2, 1791. As the end was drawing near, he murmured to Mrs. Charles Wesley, *"He giveth his servants rest;"* and as if looking by faith into the heavenly sanctuary which John [the Revelator] saw in holy vision, he would repeat, *"There is no way into the holiest but by the blood of Jesus."* A little before the end, he raised his failing arm toward heaven and exclaimed, "The best of all is, God is with us."

This story was taken from *Advance Guard of Missions* – Clifford G. Howell

Reinforce

1. Sing the hymn, "Work, for the Night Is Coming."

2. Read a book about one of the Wesleys.

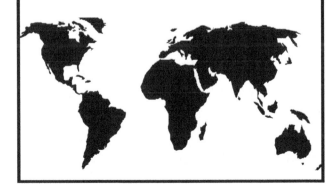

Earth and Moon

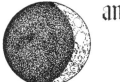

"Thick clouds are a covering to him, that he seeth not; and <u>he</u> <u>walketh</u> <u>in</u> <u>the</u> <u>circuit</u> of heaven."
Job 22:14

Planet Earth has one moon as does Pluto. Mercury and Venus have no moons. All the other planets in our solar system have two or more moons. Our moon is 2,160 miles (3,476 kilometers) in diameter. It is about 1/4 the size of the Earth's diameter. It revolves around the Earth every 29 1/2 days.

The moon *"walketh in the circuit"* as the planets move around the sun. And the sun and other stars in our solar system move around the center of the Milky Way Galaxy.

The Earth's large circle around the sun is long while the moon's trip around the Earth is short. The lesson we can learn from this is: "All our powers are to be used for Christ. This is the debt we each owe to God. In forming a relationship with Christ, the renewed man is but coming back to his appointed relationship with God. He is a representative of Christ, and he is ever to pray and watch unto prayer. <u>His duties lie around him, nigh and afar off</u>. His first duty is to his children and his <u>nearest</u> relatives. Nothing can excuse him from neglecting the <u>inner</u> <u>circle</u> [like the moon around the Earth] for the <u>larger</u> <u>circle</u> [like the Earth around the sun] <u>outside</u>."*

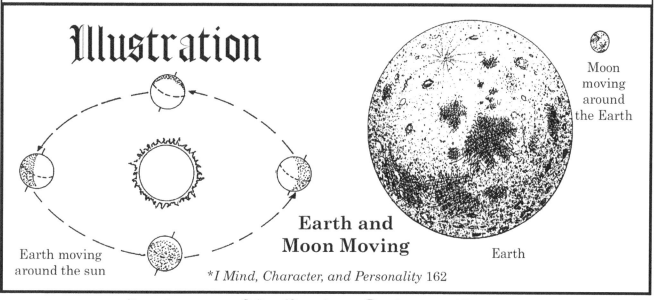

Illustration

Moon moving around the Earth

Earth and Moon Moving

Earth

Earth moving around the sun

*I Mind, Character, and Personality 162

Shape

𝕴t is he that sitteth upon the circle of the earth,
and the inhabitants thereof are as grasshoppers;
that stretcheth out the heavens as a curtain,
and spreadeth them out as a tent to dwell in."

Isaiah 40:22

God shaped the Earth like a ball—*"circle of the earth."* The North Pole is at the top and the South Pole is at the bottom. Half way between the poles and belting the Earth is an invisible line called the equator. The Earth is not perfectly round. It is somewhat flat at the poles. It is a shorter distance from pole to pole than around the equator.

"How earnestly and perseveringly the artist labors to transfer to canvas a perfect likeness of his model; and how **diligently** the sculptor hews and chisels out the stone into a counterpart of the copy he is following. So the parents should labor to shape, polish, and refine their children after the pattern given them in Christ Jesus. As the patient artist studies, and works, and forms plans to make the results of his labors more perfect, so should the parent consider time well spent that is occupied in training the children for useful lives and fitting them for the immortal kingdom. The artist's work is small and unimportant compared with that of the parent. The one deals with lifeless material, from which he fashions forms of beauty; but the other deals with a human being whose life can be shaped for good or ill, to bless humanity or to curse it; to go out in darkness, or to live forever in a future sinless world."*

"Oh, that all would understand that these small duties are not to be neglected. The whole of their future life will be shaped by the habits and practices of their childhood. Children are peculiarly susceptible to impressions, and sanitary knowledge may be imparted to them by not permitting disorder."**

Reinforce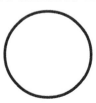

Read the thoughts, "Practice Makes Perfect."

*Child Guidance 476-477 ** Ibid 107*

Practice Makes Perfect

We had the privilege, recently, of examining a work of art by one of our best landscape painters. The first scene this artist ever put upon canvas added nothing to the value of the canvas. It was a mere daub by an inexperienced artist, and such a picture is worth no more in the market than the canvas is worth; possibly not as much. But twenty-five years of close practice has made him an expert, and his last painting is worth ten thousand dollars. The difference between ten dollars, the original price of the canvas, and ten thousand dollars, the value of his painting, is found in the quality of his work. "Practice makes perfect." What he has put upon the canvas constitutes its value now, and practice only has enabled him to do that. What is true of the fine arts is true of all the arts of work and living.

The manner of Ole Bull bringing music out of the violin was wonderful. He was the only violinist who ever aroused Edison sufficiently to note and appreciate the charm of sweet sounds, for the click of the electric battery had become the "music of the spheres" to him.

But Ole Bull, without practice, would have been a failure. He said, "If I practice one day, I can see the result; if I practice two days, my friends can see it; if three days, the great public can see it." No doubt, genius figured in his successful career, but it was through persistent practice.

The modern plan of dividing labor as to secure skill is the outcome of the idea that "practice makes perfect." Formerly one man made the gun, but now it takes about forty. Each man makes a particular part of the weapon, and does not know how to make any other part. He becomes an expert in his line, because his practice is expended upon it, and upon no other.

Edison employs three hundred and fifty hands in his works—all experts; that is, each one has become eminently skilled in his department by devoting himself to it persistently for years. He can be relied upon under all circumstances. His practice has been so thorough and has continued so long, that he stands at the head—the best there is.

A few years ago a teacher in New Haven, Connecticut, drilled two pupils in mental arithmetic until they could readily multiply twenty-one figures by twenty-one figures without recording a figure, the multiplication being entirely mental. It required forty-two figures to express the product, and yet these two students performed the elaborate mental process, and gave the result without an error, one of them being forty, and the other forty-five minutes in going through the operation. Mr. Lovell, the teacher, claimed that several of his scholars could perform the mental feat of Voltaire—multiply the nine digits by nine digits, without putting down a figure, and do it in five minutes. It was not genius, but practice that did it. Only those who aspired to superior attainments accomplished this remarkable multiplication. The youth whose ambition is content with the mental process of multiplying two or three figures by two or three figures, will never compete with the New Haven students. He lacks those qualities that enable him to surmount obstacles in the way to excellence.

Our attention was called to a boot-bottomer, who was an expert in that business.

"How many boots can you bottom in a day?" we inquired.

"Forty," he answered; "I have done more."

"How many pegs are there in a boot?"

"One hundred and five," he replied.

We computed the number of pegs he drove in a day—about eight thousand—one at a time; almost fifty thousand pegs driven in a week! Let the uninitiated ponder the work on a Monday morning—drive fifty thousand pegs, singly, by Saturday night! The task seems quite impossible! The amateur cannot accomplish the feat; it requires practice, close and long continued. This boot-bottomer had been at it from his boyhood, and the celerity and skill with which he performed his task seemed to make both hammer and pegs instinct with life. One could almost believe, on seeing him work, that a sort of intelligence characterized both hammer and pegs, fitting them exactly for their respective places. Practice did it. In the out set, his fingers were clumsy, his hammer heavy, and his motions slow and awkward. At last, his nimble fingers were suggestive of ease, his hammer was light and quick, and his movements apt and graceful. Repetition had eliminated everything with awkwardness and hesitation from his work.

At this point many persons make a mistake in their judgment of labor. That a surgeon should receive a thousand dollars for amputating a limb; a public lecturer one or two hundred dollars for a single address; an elocutionist be remunerated at the rate of fifty dollars an hour; a lawyer be paid twenty thousand dollars for conducting a suit; a preacher have a salary of ten thousand dollars; the president of a bank, railroad corporation, or insurance company, be paid twenty or thirty thousand dollars annually, and a salesman find constant employment at five or ten thousand dollars a year, many persons cannot understand. It appears to themselves enormous pay for little work. But they overlook the "practice" that "makes perfect."

Ten, twenty, and even thirty years of incessant toil preceded these positions of trust and honor. The way up to them was paved with self-denial, work, and sacrifice—the same thing over and over, year after year. Others fell out by the way. They might have enjoyed equally well-earned remuneration and distinction, but they lacked the resolution and aim to continue the "practice." Ten, twenty, or thirty years of unremitting endeavor was a monstrous lion in their way. They cowered before such an obstacle. So much practice was too large a price,

and so they do not occupy these lucrative and honorable positions; and they do not deserve them. Society, on the whole, was just and fair. It rewards practice as it does virtue, but it does not reward inaction and cowardice. The man who does his "level best" will never go begging for bread or friends. Society will do as well by him as it can, and he will have no just reason to complain.

It is practice that makes execution easy. When a man has attained to his best, his work is the most easily done. Difficulties were encountered before he reached his high standard of excellence. When he has become an expert, doing is by no means difficult. It is easy for a wise man to be wise, just as it is for a fool to be foolish.

It is easy for a really honest man to be honest, the industrious man to work, the expert to be best. Practice has run into a habit, and habit is easy.

Will Carleton, the "poet of the farm," was reared in the wilderness of Michigan, his father being one of the pioneers on what was then our frontier. He was more in love with books than he was with the farm, and his father was willing that he should be. He was allowed the best schooling that part of the country could furnish. That he was a born poet his parents never dreamed. But a public lecturer chanced to speak in that vicinity and young Carleton went to hear him. The speaker was eloquent and instructive. His young hearer was thoroughly enthused: he must become a public speaker. From that moment both poetry and prose oozed from him as readily as perspiration. The farm was nothing, but public speaking was everything. He spoke in the cornfield and woods, in the barn and stable. He addressed audiences of cattle and cornstalks, trees and fence-posts. He did it, not only daily, but several times in a day, until his father became alarmed; he feared that his son would come out at the little end of the horn, and suggested as much to him. But Will believed that practice makes perfect, and he continued the practice. Writing poetry and orating in the barn and cornfield, occupied his time more than ever. His improvement was in proportion to his practice. He practiced much and his improvement was much. At twenty-six he wrote the poem "Betsy and I Are Out," and it made him famous. Recently Mr. Carleton said, "It is a pleasant memory that my father lived to see me earning a hundred dollars a night, and admitted, with a twinkle in his eye, 'that there was more money in me than he had supposed." Practice did it.

Review Article
Place II - III

1. What does it mean "practice makes perfect?"

2. What do you practice each day to become perfect?

3. Should we only do the amount of work for which we are paid? Why or why not?

4. Read the following comments.

"Man can shape circumstances, but circumstances should not be allowed to shape the man. We should seize upon circumstances as instruments by which to work. We are to master them but should not permit them to master us.

"Men of power are those who have been opposed, baffled, and thwarted. By calling their energies into action, the obstacles they meet prove to them positive blessings. They gain self-reliance. Conflict and perplexity call for the exercise of trust in God and for that firmness which develops power.

"Christ gave no stinted service. He did not measure His work by hours. His time, His heart, His soul and strength, were given to labor for the benefit of humanity.

Through weary days He toiled, and through long nights He bent in prayer for grace and endurance that He might do a larger work. With strong crying and tears He sent His petitions to heaven, that His human nature might be strengthened, that He might be braced to meet the wily foe in all his deceptive workings, and fortified to fulfill His mission of uplifting humanity. To His workers He says, *'I have given you an example, that ye should do as I have done'* (John 13:15).

" *'The love of Christ,'* said Paul, *'constraineth us'* (II Corinthians 5:14). This was the actuating principle of his conduct; it was his motive power. If ever his ardor in the path of duty flagged for a moment, one glance at the cross caused him to gird up anew the loins of his mind and press forward in the way of self-denial. In his labors for his brethren he relied much upon the manifestation of infinite love in the sacrifice of Christ, with its subduing, constraining power.

"How earnest, how touching, his appeal: *'Ye know the grace of our Lord Jesus Christ, that, though he was rich, yet for your sakes he became poor, that ye through his poverty might be rich'* (II Corinthians 8:9). You know the height from which He stooped, the depth of humiliation to which He descended.

His feet entered upon the path of sacrifice and turned not aside until He had given His life. There was no rest for Him between the throne in heaven and the cross. His love for man led Him to welcome every indignity and suffer every abuse.

"Paul admonishes us to *'look not every man on his own things, but every man also on the things of others.'* He bids us possess the mind *'which was also in Christ Jesus: who, being in the form of God, thought it not robbery to be equal with God: but made himself of no reputation, and took upon him the form of a servant, and was made in the likeness of men: and being found in fashion as a man, he humbled himself, and became obedient unto death, even the death of the cross'* (Philippians 2:4-8)."*

The Ministry of Healing 500-501

Atmosphere

"But as he which hath called you is holy, so be ye holy in all manner of conversation."
1 Peter 1:15

Air surrounds the Earth. It goes as far as 1,000 miles (1,600 kilometers) above the crust. The air is called the atmosphere, and is made up of 78 percent nitrogen, 21 percent oxygen, 1 percent argon, and small amounts of other gases. The air also has water vapor and particles of dust and other matter. The air gets thinner as you go away from the Earth until it fades into space. These facts can teach us lessons:

"The life of Christ was an every-widening, shoreless influence, an influence that bound Him to God and to the whole human family. Through Christ, God has invested man with an influence that makes it impossible for him to live to himself. Individually we are connected with our fellow men, a part of God's great whole, and we stand under mutual obligations. No man can be independent of his fellow men; for the well-being of each affects others. It is God's purpose that each shall feel himself necessary to others' welfare, and seek to promote their happiness.

"Every soul is surrounded by an atmosphere of its own—an atmosphere, it may be, charged with the life-giving power of faith, courage, and hope, and sweet with the fragrance of love. Or it may be heavy and chill with the gloom of discontent and selfishness, or poisonous with the deadly taint of cherished sin. By the atmosphere surrounding us, every person with whom we come in contact is consciously or unconsciously affected.

"This is a responsibility from which we cannot free ourselves. Our words, our acts, our dress, our deportment, even the expression of the countenance, has an influence. Upon the impression thus made there hang results for good or evil which no man can measure. Every impulse thus imparted is seed sown which will produce its harvest. It is a link in the long chain of human events, extending we know not whither. If by our example we aid others in the development of good principles, we give them power to do good. In their turn they exert the same influence upon others, and they upon still others. Thus by our unconscious influence thousands may be blessed.

"Throw a pebble into the lake, and a wave is formed, and another and another; and as they increase, the circle widens, until it reaches the very shore. So with our influence. Beyond our knowledge or control it tells upon others in blessing or in cursing."* Our mission work is to follow the plan of the "atmosphere" and will result in a large influence for good.

Reflect

"We can surround ourselves with a sunny <u>atmosphere</u>, or with an <u>atmosphere</u> charged with gloom. Let us educate ourselves to talk courage. Let us learn lessons from the example of Christ."
Sons and Daughters of God 218

As we have described what the Earth's atmosphere is like so let us look at the chosen people and answer the question: what was their final influence? Did they have a correct understanding and knowledge about the Messiah? Did they share it with others correctly? Why? They:

• Had hopes of worldly greatness;
• Did not keep the commandments;
• Followed the ways of the heathen;
• Had heathen oppression;
• Were in apostasy;
• Were unfaithful;
• Shut themselves away from those they should have served;
• Lost sight of the real meaning of the ritual service;
• Made burdensome laws; and were
• Full of pride

Israel needed to **diligently** reform that they might have a pure atmosphere surrounding their nation to influence the world with the love of God. Are they an object lesson for us today?

"You can surround your souls with an <u>atmosphere</u> that will be like breezes from the heavenly Eden."**

*Christ's Object Lessons 339-340 **Sons and Daughters of God 180*

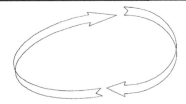

Review
Place I - II - III

1. What is a diameter? How does Earth compare with the other planets?

2. Explain the rotation of the Earth and how it moves through space.

3. Who were the Wesleys?

4. How big is the moon compared to the Earth?

5. What shape is the Earth? What spiritual lesson can we learn from this?

6. The Earth's atmosphere is made up of _____

It spiritually teaches us _____

Reinforce

1. Using family members and friends, show the three movements of the Earth. Make signs for each one to hold telling their movements (so no one will become dizzy spinning). Find a large rock to be the center of the Milky Way galaxy. Place each person in their proper spot with the proper sign. Then all gather on the rock and discuss Psalm 46:5 and Psalm 22:22.

2. Practice taking deep breaths. Thank God for Earth's atmosphere.

3. What kind of atmosphere do you have surrounding you?

Remind

1. As you are cleaning the house, washing the windows, or other chores, think how each movement of the Earth was carefully planned by God. Use your movements in work just as wisely. Be **diligent**! Who should be in the center of your thoughts as you work?

2. As you change your bed linen be reminded how God renewed the surface of the Earth at the flood and changed the ocean bed.

3. While doing outside chores consider the pure atmosphere God has placed around planet Earth.

Research
Outside and Inside the Earth

"That he would grant you, according to the riches of his glory, to be strengthened with might by his Spirit in the inner man."
Ephesians 3:16

The Outside Surface

How did the continents come into being? Did they always exist? As you perhaps already know the answer is that they did not always exist but were formed during the time of Noah's Flood. The Earth had become very wicked and God purposed to wash it and cleanse it. He would restore its fertilizing elements which had been robbed from it because the people did not allow the land her Sabbath rests. He warned the people of what He was about to do and offered them a safe refuge in the ark, but few took **diligent** heed. The fountains of the great deep were broken up and there was much volcanic activity that combined together to produce a new face on planet Earth. Thus the continents, like a new creation, arose out of the cleansing baptism of the Flood. And just as baptism is symbolic of a new life in Christ, so the Earth wore a new look after it emerged from the watery grave.

What is within comes out as the activity within the Earth helped change its surface so our thoughts and feelings affect our outward acts. "...The thoughts and feelings combined make up the moral character"* of the *"inner man."*

Foundations

Of old You Earth's foundation laid;
Your mighty hands the heavens made;
Yet they will die, while You endure.
Like garments they will worn out be;
Like clothes you change them constantly.
—*Rolland*

5 Testimonies 310

In the beginning the Earth was *"without form and void;"* so, in a sense, it was that way during the flood. But *"the Spirit of God moved upon the face of the waters"* and formed them into seas dividing the Earth into seven continents. The fact that there are seven of them indicates the spiritual perfection possible to all who will consent to be (like the continents were) *"cleansed from all unrighteousness."*

God used water, the symbolic agent of cleansing, and fire in the form of burning lava to purify the Earth and reform it. So He uses the water and fire of His word to reform and cleanse His chosen people to-day. *"We went through fire and through water: but thou broughtest us out into a wealthy place"* (Psalm 66:12). It was volcanic fire that elevated the continents. It is the fire of God's word that elevates our characters. *"Is not my word like as a fire? saith the LORD"* (Jeremiah 23:29).

The upheaval from earth-quakes during the flood and the lava floods of the volcanoes, seem-ingly destructive agents, were all under the perfect control of an om-nipotent (all-powerful) God. He used the warring elements to create the perfect number of continents. It can encourage us that He can bring order out of confused lives today. He

may use things that look like they would destroy us in the process but it is sometimes the only way to reform us.

Although the two forces of fire and water seem to work against each other, God's mighty power sustained the balance between them. Thus the ocean has not been allowed to go forth impelling its currents and rolling waves without hindrance. God asked Job, *"Where wast thou when I laid the founda-tions of the earth?...Whereupon are the foundations thereof fastened? or who laid the corner stone thereof;... Or who shut up the sea with doors, when it brake forth, as if it had is-sued out of the womb? When I made the cloud the garment thereof, and thick darkness a swaddling band for it, And brake up for it my decreed place, and set bars and doors, And said, Hitherto shalt thou come, but no further: and here shall thy proud waves be stayed?"* (Job 38:4, 6, 8-11).

The way the ocean is checked by God reminds us of the promise that *"When the enemy shall come in like a flood, the Spirit of the LORD shall lift up a standard against him"* (Isaiah 59:19). During the time of our Bible lesson Satan had **diligently** flooded the world with false ideas about God's character, but Christ would come to lift up the reputation of the Father by showing His merciful, self-sacrificing love. Today Satan has also flooded the world with false ideas about God's character, but now he is saying just the opposite of what he did in the days of Christ. He leads the multitudes to think that God is too merciful to be just and punish man for his wickedness.

The sea can remind us of God's mercy because it is like a garment that covers the low barren places of the Earth. The land can remind us how God's justice is something we can stand on and which lends stability to our lives.

Just as the sea has its limits and the land has its boundaries so does God's mercy. The story of the flood teaches us this. *"And the LORD said, My spirit shall not always strive with man"* (Genesis 6:3). God was about to quit striving with the Jewish nation. They were not cooperating with Him for the most part. God had wanted to re-form them and lift them up *"high above all nations which he hath made, in praise, and in name,"* but because of their unfaithfulness, God's justice must allow them to reap what they had sown. This meant continued adversity and humiliation.

The Lord says, *"speak to the earth, and it shall teach thee"* (Job 12:8). The continents teach us that God has boundaries to His justice and mercy. Throughout the mute language of nature with its impassable bounds of both water and land we learn of Him who *"hath measured the waters in the hollow of his hand...and comprehended the dust of the earth in a measure, and weighed the mountains in scales, and the hills in a balance"* (Isaiah 40:12). So He measures His chosen people today and determines whether the ministry of justice or mercy would best balance out their characters in each situation. Soon He is coming to cleanse the Earth with fire. Only those who measure up will be able to survive. Only His chosen people who have taken advantage of the time of mercy to form righteous characters will be able to survive the day of His justice. *"For our God is a consuming fire"* (Hebrews 12:29).

Remember, the surface of the Earth is about 70 per cent water with most of it being in the oceans. The lowest point of the Earth's surface is in the ocean and the highest point is on Mount Everest, in Asia. The lowest land is the shores of the Dead Sea.

The largest bodies of land are called continents. There are seven—Africa, Antarctica, Asia, Australia, Europe, South America, and North America. There are a perfect (7) number of continents that need to hear the perfect message of how to overcome sin and the sacrifice Jesus made for each.

Reinforce

Place I, write the names of the continents.

1. _____

2. _____

3. _____

4. _____

5. _____

6. _____

7. _____

Place II, tell your teacher the names of the 7 continents without looking.

Place III, tell the teacher the names of the continents and also spell them by writing them on the proper maps on page 56.

Earth's Crust

'Who laid the foundations of the earth, that it should not be removed for ever."
Psalm 104:5

The "skin" that covers the main body of the Earth is called the crust. The thickness of the crust goes from about 5 miles (8 kilometers) under the oceans to about 25 miles (40 kilometers) under the continents. God's people of old needed the covering of Christ's righteousness; we also need the robe of Christ's righteousness today. *"I will greatly rejoice in the LORD, my soul shall be joyful in my God; for he hath clothed me with the garments of salvation, he hath covered me with the robe of righteousness, as a bridegroom decketh himself with ornaments, and as a bride adorneth herself with her jewels"* (Isaiah 61:10).

The crust is made up of four kinds of rock: created, igneous, sedimentary, and metamorphic. Created rock was made by God in the beginning; igneous rock was formed by the slow cooling of molten rock from inside the Earth; sedimentary rock was formed by the layering of different materials; and metamorphic rocks are formed when igneous and sedimentary rocks are changed by heat and pressure. These rocks are made up of minerals. To be covered by the robe of righteousness we need to do these things;

1. Repent

2. Confess

3. Submit

4. Pray

5. Live righteous lives

What did Israel lack?

Explain?

_____

_____

_____

_____

_____

_____

_____

Reinforce
Which Continent?

You set up the Earth on foundations sure,
That always it should unshaken endure.
—*Lyons*

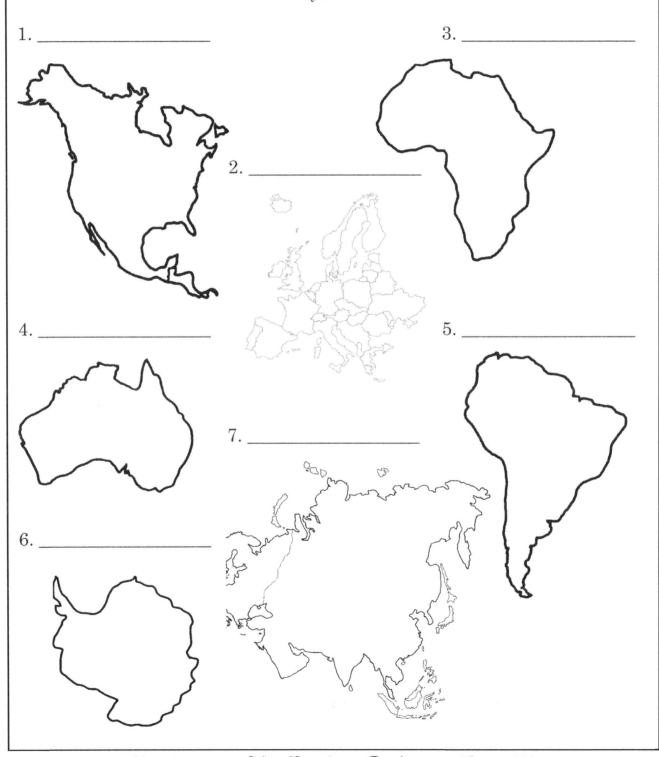

1. _____

2. _____

3. _____

4. _____

5. _____

6. _____

7. _____

Inside the Earth

'And they said one to another, Did not our <u>heart</u> <u>burn</u> <u>within</u> us, while he talked with us by the way, and while he opened to us the Scriptures?"

Luke 24:32

Beneath the Earth's crust is the mantle, the outer core, and the inner core. The following paragraphs explain what scientists believe is to be found under the crust.

The mantle is a thick layer of solid rock found beneath the crust. It goes down about 1,800 miles (2,900 kilometers). The rock of the mantle is made of silicon, oxygen, aluminum, iron, and magnesium. It is thought the temperature gradually increases going down through the mantle.

The outer core begins at about 1,800 miles (2,900 kilometers) below the Earth's surface. It is thought the outer core is about 1,400 miles (2,250 kilometers) thick and is made of melted iron and nickel. The core in the very center of the Earth and is supposed to be about 3,200 miles (5,150 kilometers) below the Earth's surface. It is thought by scientists that the core is very hot and made of solid iron and nickel. If our lives are right with Christ, our hearts will burn within us like molten rock inside the Earth.

As Israel of old so today: "The Bible has been robbed of its power, and the results are seen in a lowering of the tone of spiritual life."* "Those who are seeking the righteousness of Christ, will be dwelling upon the themes of the great salvation. The Bible is the storehouse that supplies our souls with nourishing food"** that our *"heart burn within us."*

Illustration
Inside Planet Earth

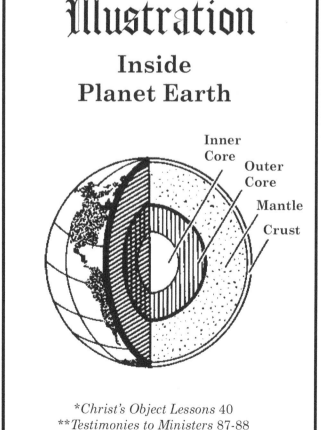

Inner Core
Outer Core
Mantle
Crust

*Christ's Object Lessons 40
**Testimonies to Ministers 87-88

Gravity

"Draw me, we will run after thee:
the king hath brought me into his chambers:
we will be glad and rejoice in thee,
we will remember thy love more than wine:
the upright love thee."
Song of Solomon 1:4

Gravity is a force that causes objects to fall when dropped. This is how God designed gravity to work in relation to planet Earth: the Earth and other planets travel around the sun because gravity pulls the planets towards the sun. Also, gravity keeps the moon traveling around the Earth. As Earth is <u>drawn</u> to the sun so we are <u>drawn</u> to God by His Holy Spirit. *"But it is good for me to <u>draw near to God</u>: I have put my trust in the Lord God, that I may declare all thy works"* (Psalm 73:28).

On the Earth, gravity keeps rivers flowing downhill and underwater soil and rocks settled.

Gravity is stronger at the poles than at the equator because the poles are closer to the Earth's center. Because of this, gravity is stronger at sea level than on mountain tops. Gravity is stronger above parts of the crust with the largest amounts of heavy rocks.

The Holy Spirit is the force or gravity that constantly <u>draws</u> us to God. How alert we need to be to hear His voice. How **diligent** to respond! Like the verse says: *"<u>Draw</u> me, we will run after thee..."*

Draw Nigh

They perish that are far from thee;
Lo, in their lewdness they shall die.
But surely it is good for me
That unto God I should <u>draw nigh</u>.
I refuge take in God the Lord,
That all thy works I may record.

Review
Place I - II - III

1. Go for a walk and find rocks, sticks and other things. Construct a picture in a shoe box of the Earth's surface or crust.

2. Draw a picture of the crust, mantle, and cores, of the inside of the Earth. Label the parts. (**Place III**, put the miles [kilometers] to show the depth of each.)

3. To observe gravity, drop a one pound (.45 kilogram) rock and one pound (.45 kilogram) of feathers (pillows), or other item at the same time.

4. Explain Isaiah 61:10-11.

Remind

1. As you do your chores like weeding, mowing, picking fruit or vegetables, notice the crust of the Earth. Think about Isaiah 61:10-11.

stammerjohan

2. Notice how we have boundaries in our lives. It can remind you about the lessons the continents and oceans teach. For example, when taking a drive, each car stays on their side of the road. Notice how people define the edges of their property with fences and hedges. Family rules are also boundaries. Once you step "over the line," the ministry of justice begins.

3. When eating bread notice the crust. Remember the earth has a crust.

Reinforce
Gravity Experiments

1. Gravity

6 ounce olive can
Cotton balls
Stepstool

• Place the can on the floor
• Place the stepstool 1 foot away from the can
• Stand on the stepstool
• Drop the cotton balls into the can

Gravity is the invisible force that pulls the light cotton ball downward toward the Earth.

2. Gravity and Weight

Small bucket with a handle
Nails, bolts, and screws

• Place some of the nails, bolts, and screws into the bucket
• Do you feel the weight? Keep adding and feel the pull on your hand and arm.
• Weight is simply the pull of the force of gravity on you or on other objects. The Earth pulls everything toward its center. The more pull gravity is able to exert on an object, is based on its denseness or mass.

3. Finding the Center of Gravity

Ruler
Pencil

• Determine the point at which the pencil balances on the edge of the ruler.

• Move the pencil about until it does not fall off. It will probably be fairly close to the eraser.

Gravity causes the needles from the pine tree to fall down to the ground.

Research
Why Did God Create the Earth?

"For thus saith the Lord that created the heavens;
God himself that formed the earth and made it;
he hath established it, he created it not in vain,
he formed it to be inhabited:
I am the Lord; and there is none else."
Isaiah 45:18

"In the beginning was the Word, and the Word was with God, and the Word was God. The same was in the beginning with God" (John 1:1-2). *"In the beginning God created the heaven and the earth"* (Genesis 1:1). *"LORD, thou hast been our dwelling place in all generations"* (Psalm 90:1).

The account of the forming of this world is found in Genesis, chapter one. "God spoke, and His words created His works in the natural world. God's creation is but a reservoir of means made ready for Him to employ instantly to do His pleasure."* *"By the word of the LORD were the heavens made; and all the host of them by the breath of his mouth." "For he spake, and it was done; he commanded, and it stood fast"* (Psalm 33:6, 9).

God made this world to make heaven larger. "He desires a larger family of created intelligences"* that could think, learn, understand, and appreciate His love.

We are told, *"For thus saith the LORD that created the heavens; God himself that formed the earth and made it; he hath established it, he created it not in vain, he formed it to be inhabited: I am the LORD; and there is none else."* He said, *"Be fruitful and multiply"* (Genesis 1:22, 28).

"In the creation it was His purpose that the Earth be inhabited by beings whose existence should be a blessing to themselves and to one another, and an honor to their Creator. All who will may identify themselves with this purpose. Of them it is spoken, *'This people have I formed for myself; they shall show forth my praise'* (Isaiah 43:21)."**

*I Bible Commentary 1081 **Education 174

Why Did God Create Man

"And God said, Let us make man in our image, after our likeness: and let them have dominion over the fish of the sea, and over the fowl of the air, and over the cattle, and over all the earth, and over every creeping thing that creepeth upon the earth."

Genesis 1:26

Remember how "All heaven took a deep and joyful interest in the creation of the world and of man. Human beings were a new and distinct order. They were made *'in the image of God,'* and it was the Creator's design that they should populate the earth."*

"And God said, Let us make man in our image, after our likeness: and let them have dominion over the fish of the sea, and over the fowl of the air, and over the cattle, and over all the earth, and over every creeping thing that creepeth upon the earth" (Genesis 1:26).

"And the LORD God formed man of the dust of the ground, and breathed into his nostrils the breath of life; and man became a living soul" (Genesis 2:7).

"God created man for His own glory, that after test and trial the human family might become one with the heavenly family. It was

God's purpose to repopulate heaven with the human family, if they would show themselves obedient to His every word. Adam was to be tested, to see whether he would be obedient, as the loyal angels, or disobedient. If he stood the test, his instruction to his children would have been only of loyalty. His mind and thoughts would have been as the mind and thoughts of God. He would have been taught by God as His husbandry and building. His character would have been moulded in accordance with the character of God."*

Man was to be **diligent** in glorifying God in his thoughts, words, and acts.

*I Bible Commentary 1081-1082

How the Earth Changed
"And the waters prevailed upon the earth a hundred and fifty days."
Genesis 7:24

"As the Earth came forth from the hand of its Maker, it was exceedingly beautiful. Its surface was diversified with mountains, hills, and plains, interspersed with noble rivers and lovely lakes; but the hills and mountains were not abrupt and rugged, abounding in terrific steeps and frightful chasms, as they now do; the sharp, ragged edges of earth's rocky framework were buried beneath the fruitful soil, which everywhere produced a luxuriant growth of verdure. There were no loathsome swamps or barren deserts. Graceful shrubs and delicate flowers greeted the eye at every turn. The heights were crowned with trees more majestic than any that now exist. The air, untainted by foul miasma, was clear and healthful. The entire landscape outvied in beauty the decorated grounds of the proudest palace. The angelic host viewed the scene with delight, and rejoiced at the wonderful works of God."*

"As man came forth from the hand of his Creator, he was of lofty stature and perfect symmetry. His countenance bore the ruddy tint of health and glowed with the light of life and joy. Adam's height was much greater than that of men who now inhabit the Earth. Eve was somewhat less in stature; yet her form was noble, and full of beauty. The sinless pair wore no artificial garments; they were clothed with a covering of light and glory, such as the angels wear. So long as they lived in obedience to God, this robe of light continued to enshroud them."**

"The creation was now complete. *'The heavens and the earth were finished, and all the host of them.' 'And God saw everything that he had made, and, behold, it was very good.'* Eden bloomed on earth. Adam and Eve had free access to the tree of life. No taint of sin or shadow of death marred the fair creation. *'The morning stars sang together, and all the sons of God shouted for joy'* (Job 38:7).

"The great Jehovah had laid the foundations of the Earth; He had dressed the whole world in the garb of beauty and had filled it with things useful to man; He had created all the wonders of the land and of the sea. In six days the great

*Patriarchs and Prophets 44 **Ibid 45*

work of creation had been accomplished. And God *'rested on the seventh day from all his work which he had made. And God blessed the seventh day, and sanctified it: because that in it he had rested from all his work which God created and made.'* God looked with satisfaction upon the work of His hands. All was perfect, worthy of its divine Author, and He rested, not as one weary, but as well pleased with the fruits of His wisdom and goodness and the manifestations of His glory.

"After resting upon the seventh day, God sanctified it, or set it apart, as a day of rest for man. Following the example of the Creator, man was to rest upon this sacred day, that as he should look upon the heavens and the Earth, he might reflect upon God's great work of creation; and that as he should behold the evidences of God's wisdom and goodness, his heart might be filled with love and reverence for his Maker."*

So why has the Earth changed so much from the beautiful description given here? Sin! Just three letters, S I N. What is sin? (Notice the "I" between the "S" and the "N." And the first and last letter of Satan is "S" and "N.")

"Whosoever committeth sin transgresseth also the law: for sin is the transgression of the law" (I John 3:4).

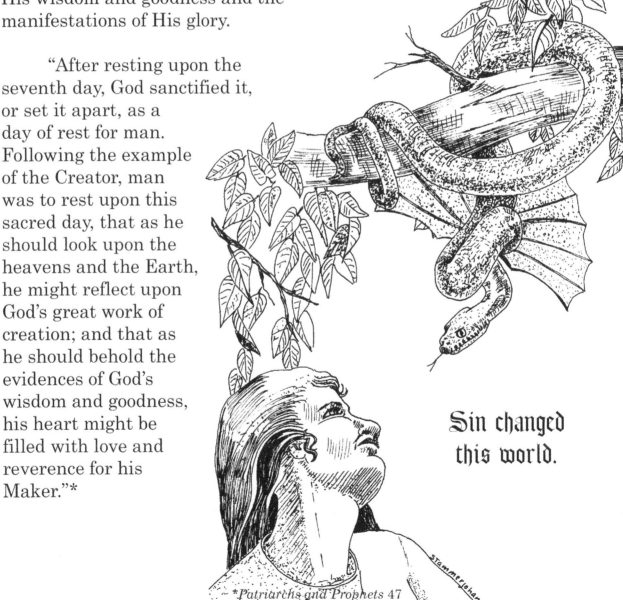

Sin changed
this world.

*Patriarchs and Prophets 47

Adam and Eve chose their own way instead of God's way. They were not **diligent** in obeying His word. We can read about what happened in Genesis 3. It seemed like such a small thing, just a piece of fruit! But it changed this whole world and the people who live on it.

We are told these sad words, *"And God saw that the wickedness of man was great in the earth, and that every imagination of the thoughts of his heart was only evil continually.*

"And it repented the LORD that he had made man on the earth, and it grieved him at his heart.

"And the LORD said, I will destroy man whom I have created *from the face of the earth; both man, and beast, and the creeping thing, and the fowls of the air; for it repenteth me that I have made them.*

"But Noah found grace in the eyes of the LORD" (Genesis 6:5-8).

The sin of Eve brought great spiritual changes in man as the Flood brought physical changes to the face of the Earth. Read these descriptions about the Earth:

"The entire surface of the Earth was changed at the Flood. A third dreadful curse rested upon it in consequence of sin. As the water began to subside, the hills and mountains were surrounded by a vast, turbid sea, Everywhere were strewn the dead bodies of men and beasts. The Lord would not permit these to remain to decompose and pollute the air, therefore He made of the Earth a vast burial ground. A violent wind which was caused to blow for the purpose of drying up the waters, moved them with great force, in some instances even carrying away the tops of the mountains and heaping up trees, rocks, and Earth above the bodies of the dead. By the same means the silver and gold, the choice wood and precious stones, which had enriched and adorned the world before the Flood, and which the inhabitants had idolized, were concealed from the sight and search of men, the violent action of the waters piling Earth and rocks upon these treasures, and in some cases even forming mountains above them. God saw that the more He enriched and prospered sinful men, the more they would corrupt their ways before Him. The treasures that should have led them to glorify the bountiful Giver had been worshiped, while God had been dishonored and despised.

"The Earth presented an appearance of confusion and desolation impossible to describe. The mountains, once so beautiful in their perfect symmetry, had become broken and irregular. Stones, ledges, and ragged rocks were now scattered upon the surface of the Earth. In many places hills and mountains had disappeared, leaving no trace where they once stood; and plains had given place to mountain ranges. These changes were more marked in some places than in others.

"Where once had been Earth's richest treasures of gold, silver, and precious stones, were seen the heaviest marks of the curse. And upon countries that were not inhabited, and those where there had been the least crime, the curse rested more lightly."*

When it was time for Jesus to come to this Earth sin had even changed His chosen people. Let us be **diligent** in being faithful to Him; then, the only change will be to be like Jesus.

Reinforce

1. Sing the hymn, "I Would Be Like Jesus."

2. On a nature walk look for the results of the Flood.

3. Find creatures in nature that obey the command, *"Be fruitful and multiply."*

Remind

As we plant flowers in our yards and keep them weeded, remember with what **diligence** we need to keep our hearts beautified. We can be careful of our thoughts words and acts. It will remind us also of some of the beauty of the Earth before the Flood.

Earth an Eden

Little drops of water,
Little grains of sand,
Make the mighty ocean,
And the beauteous land;
Little deeds of kindness,
Little words of love,
Make our Earth an Eden,
Like the Heaven above.

—Unknown

Remainder
History of the Earth

"The law of the Lord is perfect
converting the soul:
the testimony of the Lord
is sure,
making wise the simple."
Psalm 19:7

The history of the Earth is recorded in three basic places:

1. **Bible,**

2. **Nature,**

3. **And the lives of people.**

(1) The Bible is one witness God left us, that we might never be confused about the history of the Earth.

(2) Nature yet witnesses to the lingering beauty of Eden before sin. It also tells us of the story of the destruction of the Flood.

(3) Finally, the lives of the righteous, witness of life everlasting to all who are **diligent** in overcoming. But sure destruction will come to all who are continuing in their sins. Unrighteous lives continue to witness to us of Eden lost and the final consequence of sin.

Law

Jehovah's perfect law
Restores the soul again;
His testimony sure
Gives wisdom unto men;
The precepts of the Lord are right,
And fill the heart with great delight.

God's word says, *"the testimony of the LORD is sure, making wise the simple"* (Psalm 19:7). *"Thy word have I hid in mine heart, that I might not sin against thee"* (Psalm 119:11).

Thy word I've treasured in my heart,
That I give no offense to Thee.
Thou, O Jehovah, blessed art;
Thy statutes teach Thou unto me.
—*L.M. Hesperus*

As we are **diligent** to follow God's words in our lives we will be a witness to all around us. We can be part of "His Chosen People" today.

In future lessons we will learn more about History, Geography, and Prophecy concerning planet Earth.

Reinforce

1. We witness through missions. Read the story, "Big Bill."

2. What is History? What is Geography? What is Prophecy?

'If he have faith,
the believer
cannot be restrained.
He betrays himself.
He breaks out. He confesses
and teaches this gospel to the
people at the risk
of life itself."
Martin Luther

Big Bill

In the corner of a tiny church in Maine sat a group of boys waiting for their church-school teacher. They were boys whose fathers worked in a lumber-camp near by. They had big, strong bodies and ruddy complexions. When they heard that a real missionary was coming to the church, they sent Big Bill, their leader, to the superintendent to ask if he might teach their class. No teacher every stayed long with that class of boys, and they needed a new substitute.

As they sat talking about the questions they intended to ask him, the superintendent entered the room with the missionary. He was tall, thin, gray-haired and very pale.

"Look at him!" said Mike, the mischief-maker. "He never could hunt elephants or tigers in Africa."

"Or fight with men who wanted to kill him, like our book said John G. Paton did," said Big Bill.

"I ain't going to stay and listen to a white-faced man like that," said Tom.

"Then let's stay and have some fun with him," said Mike. So, with minds that were full of mischief, the boys waited for the missionary to come to their class.

"Every red-blooded boy likes to read and hear stories of fights and hunts," said the missionary, a few moments later, pulling his chair up close to Mike's, "so I am going to tell you a little about three hunts that I have seen within a year, and then let you ask me questions. Look at these pictures first," and he drew three from his pocket.

Every boy was on the edge of his chair in a minute, for the first picture was one of a great lion with shaggy mane, lying dead at the feet of some big African men, and having a long spear stuck into his side.

"This old fellow had stolen three little children from one of our African towns before the men finally succeeded in driving him into a place where they could kill him," said the missionary, and then he described the lion-hunt.

"And this old witch-doctor," he continued, holding up a picture of a ragged, ugly, painted man, "was hired by the village to hunt for a woman whom they might put to death for being a witch. One of the head men in the town had died and they were sure some one had bewitched him. This witch-doctor chose a mother who lived far away and who knew nothing about the man's death, but he tortured her until she said that she was a witch and had killed the man." Then he told them about that witch-hunt, and how he had saved the life of the woman.

"Now this boy," he said, holding up a picture of a fine-looking African boy about the size of the boys in the class, "was hunted by men with spears because his own father wanted to kill him. Chivela had become a Christian, and his father would rather see him dead than to see him change his religion. He put poison in the boy's food; he tried to make him fall into a trap. Finally Chivela ran away from home into the woods, and had to hide in caves for many days to get away from the men whom his father had hired to kill him."

"Chivela walked nearly a hundred miles before he reached the school where I am a teacher," continued the missionary. "He lived on raw fruits and the flesh of little animals which he could kill with his knife. Chivela wanted to go to school, so he has been working hard for three years to pay his own way. He isn't one bit afraid of his

father now, and he wants to go home next year and try to win him for Christ."

For a few moments it seemed as though every boy in the class wanted to ask questions all at once about that big lion or the witch-doctor or the schoolboy. Suddenly Big Bill, who had been very quiet during the story of all three hunts, said:

"I should like to know what a boy has to do if he wants to be a missionary. I thought missionaries had to preach and have church school, but I liked that story of John G. Paton which I have just read, and now I like your story. That's the king of life I should like to live."

After a little discussion as to what the boys thought a missionary was like, the man told them how the Boards required that a young Christian volunteer be well in body and have a good education and good habits; how he must be recommended highly, and have a big desire to work for God in any field to which he might be sent, if they were to invest money in him and send him to the Mission field.

When the bell rang the boys were sorry, for they had enjoyed the hour, and they had learned much that they did not know about missionaries and their work.

"Hm-m-m!" said Big Bill to himself as he walked home. "I hain't finished our school here. I don't have very good habits, but I'm not afraid and I'm well. That is something. I think I'd like to be a missionary, if I can."

The next day Big Bill began to try to stop swearing. " 'Cause I think a missionary oughtn't to do it," he said to himself. When the men laughed at him and tried to make him angry so that he would swear, he would think of the African boy, Chivela, and grit his teeth. He tried to be more kind about the lumber-camp. One day he pulled out the Testament which had been given to him in a city Sabbath school many years before, and began to try to find out what Jesus was like, and what he wanted a boy to be and do.

Big Bill had always been a good story-teller, and he could tell the story of the lion-hunt in a way that made the boys shiver as they listened to it. When the men sat about the camp fire at night they would often ask him to tell them a story. Sometimes he told of the lion or the witch-doctor, but sometimes he told one of the stories which he had read in his Testament—the

cleansing of the temple, the feeding of the five thousand, or the stilling of the storm. Big Bill could make those stories live. Only to his mother had he confided that some day he hoped to be a missionary, but all who knew him realized that something very real had happened to Big Bill.

That fall Big Bill asked to be allow to go back to school, although he was almost a man compared with the little ones who attended the school in the village nearest the lumber-camp. The children made fun of his mistakes, and sometimes he found it very hard to stick to his purpose. But whenever he wanted to turn coward, he said to himself, "Chivela wouldn't do that," and he stuck to his work.

In five years he had finished the high school with good grades and wanted to go to college. The minister in the church where he had been trying to help during his high-school course had told him where to write, but when September came, he had had no word of an opportunity to study and at the same time to earn money. However, William, as he was now called by his school friends, had become so well acquainted with the life of Jesus that he was banking on the value of work and prayer to open a way. He had written many letters, and day after day he prayed that some one would need him. Then one day a wonderful letter came—at least it seemed wonderful to the boy:

"We have only one place in which we could use you," it said. "Some one has to keep the furnaces going in the fall and winter, and work in the gardens in the spring. There is a large quantity of coal and ashes to handle, but if you care to do this, it will pay for your board and tuition. There is a room in the basement which is not very attractive, but which some students in the past have chosen to use. You are welcome to the use of it if you decide to tend the furnaces. If you are strong and well, and if you have good habits, we shall be glad to have you come, and we will do our best to help you get the education which you so much desire."

"Strong and well, and with good habits," said William. "That's part of what the Mission Boards expect. Well, this time I can say that I have some good habits, and I am still well and strong." So he went to college and shoveled coal to pay for it.

Four years later he was graduated with honor and with fine recommendations for character and service. That fall William La Crosse sailed for the foreign field, a missionary of the Cross.

"Off for a lion-hunt or a fight against a witch-doctor, perhaps," he said, laughingly, to a group of his friends who knew what it was that had created his desire to be a missionary. "If that fight with the lion is any harder than the fight I have had with myself to get ready to go, it will take some courage to win it. I can show you now how the first fight came out. When I come back in five or six years, watch me try to find a group of boys away back in my little old town in Maine and tell them about some other fights."

Reflect

Another word for **diligence** is "effort."

"Elbow-grease is the best polish."
—*English Proverb*

"Much effort, much prosperity."
—*Euripides, c. 421 B.C.*

"Few things are impossible to **diligence** and skill."
—*Samuel Johnson, 1759*

Review
Final
Place I - II – III

1. Teacher, dictate the spelling words. Define the spelling words.

2. Why did God make this world?

3. Read Genesis 1.

4. What was special about man?

5. What changed the appearance of the Earth?

6. Draw two pictures of scenery—one before the Flood and one after the Flood. Color your pictures. Or build a picture from other pictures of these two scenes.

7. Our lives can be beautiful like the world was before the Flood. How? **Diligent** is a key word in the answer.

Reinforce
Make Planet Earth

1.
A. Make a world out of paper mache or a blue ball.

B. Use green or brown paper to cut out the seven continents. Use a map to trace or copy from to get the right shape. Copy the right name on each continent. Glue these on the sphere.

2. Do the Bible Mark, "About Early Geography."

3. Read the poems, "Planet Earth," and "The Wonderful World."

4. Sing the hymn, "From Greenland's Icy Mountains."

Remind

1. As you watch the bread dough rise and get larger, remember how God wanted to enlarge heaven, so He made man.

2. Is there some way you can help God to enlarge heaven? (Example: Praying for and witnessing to others.)

3. When seeing a beautiful nature scene think of what the Earth once looked like, the Garden of Eden.

Planet Earth

Many Answers to One Question

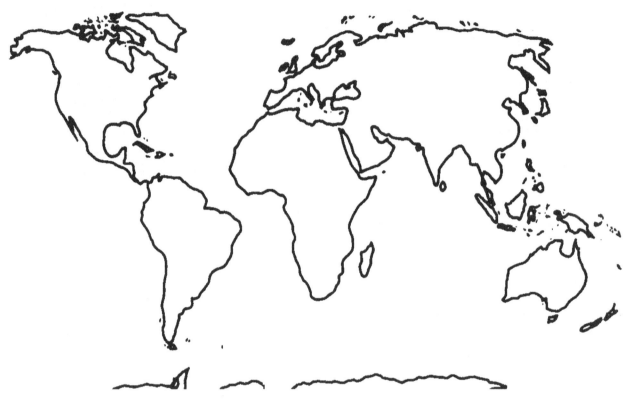

What is Earth, school-boy?
    A place for my play;
What is Earth, maiden?
    A place to be a ray;
What is Earth, mourner?
    A place where I weep;
What is Earth, sluggard?
    A good place to sleep;
What is Earth, soldier?
    A place for battles;
What is Earth, herdsman?
    A place to raise cattle;
What is Earth, widow?
    A place of true sorrow;
What is Earth, tradesman?
    I'll tell you to-morrow;

What is Earth, sick man?
    'Tis nothing to me;
What is Earth, sailor;
    My home is the sea;
What is Earth, statesman?
    A place to win fame;
What is Earth, author?
    I'll write there my name;
What is Earth, monarch?
    For my realm 'tis given;
What is Earth, Christian?
    The gateway to Heaven!

—*Unknown*

Mark Your Bible

About Early Geography

1. Of what two things was the earth made when it was first created?

"And God said, Let the waters under the heaven be gathered together unto one place, and let the dry land appear: and it was so" (Genesis 1:9).

2. From what were the land and water made?

"Through faith we understand that the worlds were framed by the word of God, so that things which are seen were not made of things which do appear" (Hebrews 11:3).

3. How were they created?

"By the word of the LORD were the heavens made; and all the host of them by the breath of his mouth.... For he spake, and it was done; he commanded, and it stood fast" (Psalm 33:6, 9).

4. What was the condition of the land and water on the first day?

The land was completely covered with water.

"And the earth was without form, and void; and darkness was upon the face of the deep. And the Spirit of God moved upon the face of the waters....And God said, Let the waters under the heaven be gathered together unto one place, and let the dry land appear: and it was so" (Genesis 1:2, 9).

5. What was the result of the gathering of the waters?

The dry land appeared. (See Genesis 1:9 on the answer to #4.)

6. What did God call the waters which He had gathered together? and what did He call the dry land?

"And God called the dry land Earth; and the gathering together of the waters called he Seas..." (Genesis 1:10).

7. Has the dry land ever been covered with water since the third day?

See Genesis 6-8.

It was covered with water at the time of the flood, in the days of Noah.

8. Was it hard work for the Lord to lift up the dry land to form continents and islands?

"Behold, the nations are as a drop of a bucket, and are counted as the small dust of the balance: behold, he taketh up the isles as a very little thing" (Isaiah 40:15).

9. Was it God's original purpose that the waters should overflow the land?

"When he gave to the sea his decree, that the waters should not pass his commandment: when he appointed the foundations of the earth" (Proverbs 8:29).

10. What sign has God given that the earth will not be destroyed again by a flood?

"And I will establish my covenant with you; neither shall all flesh be cut off any more by the waters of a flood; neither shall there any more be a flood to destroy the earth....I do set my bow in the cloud, and it shall be for a token of a covenant between me and the earth" (Genesis 9:11, 13).

Reinforce
Sing the hymn, "All Things Bright and Beautiful."

"All things bright and beautiful, All creatures great and small,
All things wise and wonderful, The Lord God made them all.

"The purple headed mountain, The river running by,
The sunset, and the morning That brightens up the sky."

—Cecil F. Alexander

The Wonderful World

Great, wide, wonderful, beautiful world,
With the beautiful water above you curled,
And the wonderful grass upon your breast—
World, you are beautifully dressed!

The wonderful air is over me,
And the wonderful wind is shaking the tree;
It walks on the water and whirls the mills,
And talks to itself on the tops of the hills.

You friendly earth, how far do you go,
With wheat fields that nod, and rivers that flow,
And cities and gardens, and oceans and isles,
And people upon you for thousands of miles?

Ah, you are so great and I am so small,
I hardly can think of you, world, at all;
And yet, when I said my prayers today,
A whisper within me seemed to say:
"You are more than the earth, though you're such a dot;
You can love and think, and the world cannot."
—Unknown

Reflect

Rejoice

Let heaven and Earth and seas rejoice,
Let all therein give praise,
For Zion God will surely save,
Her broken walls will raise.

In Zion they that love His Name
Shall dwell from age to age;
yea, there shall be their lasting rest,
Their children's heritage.

—C.M. Balerma

Outline of School Program

Age	Grade	Program
Birth through Age 7	Babies Kindergarten and Pre-school	*Family Bible Lessons* (This includes: Bible, Science–Nature, and Character)
Age 8	First Grade	*Family Bible Lessons* (This includes: Bible, Science–Nature, and Character) + Language Program (*Writing and Spelling Road to Reading and Thinking* [WSRRT])
Age 9-14 or 15	Second through Eighth Grade	*The Desire of all Nations* (This includes: Health, Mathematics, Music, Science–Nature, History/Geography/Prophecy, Language, and Voice–Speech) + Continue using WSRRT
Ages 15 or 16-19	Ninth through Twelfth Grade	9 – *Cross and Its Shadow I** + Appropriate Academic Books 10 – *Cross and Its Shadow II** + Appropriate Academic Books 11 – *Daniel the Prophet** + Appropriate Academic Books 12 – *The Seer of Patmos** (Revelation) + Appropriate Academic Books **or you could continue using* The Desire of Ages
Ages 20-25	College	Apprenticeship

Made in the USA
Monee, IL
21 August 2022

11941362R00063